THE PRIMACY OF EXISTENCE
IN THOMAS AQUINAS

THE PRIMACY
OF EXISTENCE
IN THOMAS AQUINAS

A Commentary in
Thomistic Metaphysics

by Dominic Banez

TRANSLATION WITH AN INTRODUCTION
AND NOTES
BY BENJAMIN S. LLAMZON

WYTHE-NORTH
PUBLISHING

Originally published in 1966.
Reprint rights granted by the estate of Benjamin S. Llamzon.
This volume is unabridged.

Translated from
*Scholastica Commentaria in Primam Partem Angelici Doctoris
ad Sexagesimam Quartem Questionem, Salmanticae 1584.*

Library of Congress Catalog Card No. 66-26972

ISBN-13: 978-0-9907386-3-3

10 9 8 7 6 5 4 3 2 1

Wythe-North Publishing
P.O. Box 1208
Proctorville, Ohio 45669

INTRODUCTION

1. **Life.** Dominic Banez was born February 29, 1528.
While one can find references to both Medina del
Campo and Valladolid in Spain as Banez' birthplace,
it is fairly certain that the latter is the correct place.
Dominic was the youngest of seven children born to
Juan Banez and Francisca Lopez. Not long after the
birth of her youngest child, Francisca Banez died.
Dominic's father remarried, and the family settled
at Medina del Campo. There Juan Banez came to be
called "The Mondragonnian," [1] an appellation which
his son Dominic seemed happy to inherit.

In 1542, Banez, already well-versed in Latin at
the age of fifteen, began his liberal arts studies in
Salamanca. His fellow-students there were men of
outstanding talents, many of whom eventually
achieved eminence. When he completed his studies
in 1546, Dominic joined the Order of Preachers, a
step he had anticipated since boyhood. He made his
profession at St. Stephen, the Dominican house of
studies at Salamanca, on May 3, 1547. He thought
himself fortunate to have studied here under such
brilliant teachers as Melchior Cano, Dominic de
Soto, and other thinkers who in turn had studied

under the renowned Francisco de Vitoria. Eventually Banez himself formed a link in the line of tradition from Vitoria.

After profession, Banez spent some years at St. Stephen. He and the gifted Bartholomew de Medina served as tutors to the younger members of the Order under the supervision of an *optimus praeceptor,* probably Diego de Chaves. On October 23, 1549, Banez qualified to be a member of *Students of Cajetan,* an elite organization at Salamanca. He became Master of Students in St. Stephen and lectured on St. Thomas' *Summa Theologiae.* He was appointed a substitute for absent professors, a recognition of professional ability then. In 1561, he lectured on the Master of the Sentences *pro forma et gradu magisterii* after which he received his doctorate in Sacred Theology at the University of Siguenza. He went to Avila in January, 1565, and taught there until 1567. From 1567 to 1569, he was a substitute teacher in theology at the University of Alcala, where he was promoted to Prefect of Studies in 1569. At the end of the following year he returned to Salamanca to lecture on the third part of the *Summa.* In June, 1571, the Dominican general chapter in Rome granted a request submitted by the provincial chapter in Santa Maria de Nieva that Banez be given the *Magistracy* in Sacred Theology. The next year he was elected Vice-Rector of the University of Salamanca. Between 1573 and 1577 he also held an administrative position in the Inquisition. More than once he was elected to head other Dominican houses even when it seemed physically impossible for him to assume another post. On April 20, 1577, he won appointment to the chair of Durandus at the University of Salamanca. Finally, upon the death of Bartholomew de Medina, he succeeded to the highest chair of the University. He held this prestigious post continually until 1600. In accordance with orders from the Dominican general, Banez began formal publication of his writings in 1584. He died at the Dominican convent in Medina on November 12, 1604, at the age of seventy-six.

At the peak of his career Banez' influence was felt in almost every position of importance in Spain. He is known to historians chiefly as the formidable foe of the Jesuit Molina on the question of divine causality and human freedom. This controversy, however, was only a segment of a whole spectrum of interests which Banez pursued intensely throughout his life. He profited from the rugged constitution typical of his fellow Basques as he maintained his activities at fever pitch. He was adviser and confidant of Philip II and a member of the Inquisitorial commission. St. Teresa of Avila had complete confidence in Banez as her spiritual guide. Besides assuming the vice-rectorship and the top academic post at Salamanca, he was superior at St. Stephen. He was invited to the important chapters of his order and engaged energetically in the *De Auxiliis* controversy. In the midst of these activities he produced a deskful of books on various branches of theology and philosophy and wrote a recommendation for the establishment of a world court to settle international disputes. He also helped in drawing up the Gregorian calendar. He was known in Spain as *praeclarissimum jubar,* his country's brightest light.

II. **Works.** Banez' works are, for the most part, commentaries on St. Thomas' *Summa Theologiae.* They are as follows:[2]

1571-72	In III, QQ. 1-42.
1579-80	In III, QQ. 60-62; 8-16; Supplement. Also the tracts: *De Censuris in Communi; De Potestate Clavium; De Excommunicatione.*
1582	*Contra Reliquia Pelagianorum Censurae.*
1583-84	In I-II, QQ. 1-18.
1584	In I, QQ. 1-64; In II-II, (*De Fide, Spe, et Charitate*).
1585	Commentary *De Generatione et Corruptione.*
1588	In I, QQ. 65 on.

1589-90   In III, QQ. 1-8.
1590-91   In III, QQ. 9-19.
1590   *Relectio de Merito et Augmento Charitatis.*
1591-93   In III, QQ. 62-68.
1593-94   In III, QQ. 84-90; Supplement QQ. 1-8.
1594   Commentary *De Iusitia et Iure.*
1598-99   In I-II, QQ. 81-89.
1599   *Institutiones Minoris Dialecticae.*
1599-1600   In I-II, QQ. 109-114.

III. **Banez' Metaphysics of Existence in the XVI Century.** If we consider the shift in perspective from object to the thinking subject and into the conditions which structure subjective consciousness as the highlight of the "Copernican revolution" of modern philosophy, we can readily appreciate the significance of Suarezian metaphysics as *the* metaphysics Descartes and Kant knew prior to their own moments of creative originality.[3] Against Suarez and his school (to which Molina, whom Banez opposed in the *De Auxiliis* controversy, belonged) Banez insisted on a return to the authentic teaching of Aquinas on the primacy of the act of existing over the so-called eternal, immutable, and necessary essences. In point of fact, the struggle over the question of divine causality and human freedom, with all attendant risks and assurances, imagined or real, involved a difference on a profounder level, in the metaphysics out of which the conflicting positions issued.[4] Banez felt sure, and said so repeatedly, that his doctrine reflected Aquinas' teaching. The claim was dismissed, however, and the alternative consequences of an existence metaphysics could not be effectively exploited later on at several turning points in modern philosophy. Instead, an essentialistic scholasticism gained general acceptance and pushed its tide towards La Flèche and Königsberg.

In the metaphysical treatise translated here, we see an effort in the late sixteenth century to pit an esse metaphysics against an essence metaphysics which even then had overwhelming historical forces on its side. A long line of schoolmen had prepared the way for Suarez. Duns Scotus' understanding of being in terms of forms loomed large in Suarez' mind. Before Scotus, the controversy between Giles of Rome and Henry of Ghent gave birth to what Fabro has called "bastard expressions in Thomism," *esse essentiae* and *esse existentiae*. As though the mere coupling of the words were not ghastly enough, the expressions solidified into stock phrases of metaphysical discourse and remained in general use for an unbelievably long time.[5] As this essentialistic account of being shaped itself into a tradition, Aquinas' understanding of being as the first and fundamental act by which every other metaphysical principle is made real was forgotten. At best, existence was taken for the bare fact, the being-there, the state of actual essence as distinguished from the state of possible essence through the intervention of efficient causality.[6] At worst, existence was tolerated as a troublesome intruder which nevertheless had to be shown in, assigned a place, and then quickly "reduced" to the status of essences. Nor is that view any happier which would avoid these extremes by holding a parity between essence and esse or would understand an esse metaphysics as an "inverted essentialism." Philosophical reflection which is riveted upon the act of being eventually grasps epistemology, philosophy of man, ethics, etc., from a perspective irreducibly different in method from that of a system centered on the limits and kinds of being as first principles.

Even Banez himself made a concession regarding the real distinction between essence and existence. His use of the distorted phrases we just discussed tends to "give pause" even to one inclined to credit him with the "deepest understanding" of St. Thomas' doctrine among all the commentators.[7] Nevertheless, a reading of the definitive position which is presented here shows that he unequivocally rejected the essentialistic interpretations of Aquinas' metaphysics prevailing in his day. Here he records his dissatisfaction with the deceptive notion propounded by Cajetan of esse as "ultimate act." He insists on Aquinas' teaching that esse is *first act by which* anything is real at all. Esse, he says, is not substance, nor is it an accident. It is not an essential constituent, nor in any way to be understood as a classification among the predicaments. Esse transcends all these; it is the act by which any of these causes *are* causes. Thus, in a finite being, esse, though extrinsic to the creature's essence, is yet the most internal to it of all the principles. Essence relates to esse only as a limit, and the very reality of that limit is from esse. Clearly, we are encountering here a metaphysics of a far different cut from that of Aristotle or Suarez.

Unheeded in his times, Banez' commentaries are now considered the best presentation of Aquinas' teaching and "indispensable reading" for anyone who wishes to orient himself along Aquinas' view of being.[8] It is interesting to see contemporary thinkers who draw inspiration from Aquinas probe the realities of person, freedom, responsibility, knowledge, etc.,[9] in continuity with a metaphysics first thought out in the 1200's, then gradually lost, then briefly and unsuccessfully upheld at a critical moment in the history of metaphysical thought in the late 1500's.

*   *   *

Here it may be well to mention the purpose of this translation. When a teacher uses the historical approach in his metaphysics classes, at the same time that his own persuasions tend to synthesize along the lines of an esse metaphysics, there is the problem of getting a text that is effective, yet brief enough to balance out with selections from other schools of thought. This Banez commentary can perhaps be such a text when the time comes to discuss the metaphysical tradition from Aquinas. The translation was done with this possibility in mind. After drafting a literal translation, each sentence was recast to make it as readable as possible to present-day students. No book in classroom use today uses the schoolman's mode of presentation which Banez used, namely, point to be proven, followed by the syllogistic proof, followed in turn by another syllogism proving the major premise, the minor, etc. Hence, I have not followed that structure in all its technicalities. Needless to say, I am not unmindful of corrections or alternate renditions Latin scholars could suggest for various parts of this difficult commentary. However, I feel that, for all its imperfections, the translation bears the insights of the original without betrayal.

For their assistance in various ways I am grateful to the following: Reverend Maurice R. Holloway, S.J., Reverend Louis Peinado, S.J., Sister Mary Anne, B.V.M., my wife Shirley; the librarians at Cudahy Library, Loyola University, at Albertus Magnus Lyceum, River Forest, Illinois, and at St. Mary of

the Lake Seminary, Mundelein, Illinois; Janice Good-
man and Mary Ann Makowski of the Henry Regnery
Company.

BENJAMIN S. LLAMZON
Loyola University
Chicago

THE PRIMACY OF EXISTENCE
IN THOMAS AQUINAS

THE TEXT
OF THOMAS AQUINAS †

WHETHER ESSENCE AND EXISTENCE ARE THE SAME IN GOD

Perhaps essence and existence (esse) are not the same in God for the following reasons:

First, if they are the same, then nothing is added to the divine existence. Now the existence to which no addition is made is existence as commonly predicated of all things. God then would be existence as commonly predicable of all things. But this is false. "Men gave an incommunicable name to stones and wood," says the Book of Wisdom, XIV, 21.

Second, as was said above (q. 2, a. 2), we can know whether God exists, but we cannot know *what He is. Therefore, God's existence is not the same as His essence, whatness, or nature.*

On the contrary, Hilary says in Book VII On The Trinity (PL 10,208) *"Existence is not an accident in*

† Translated from the Leonine edition of *Summa Theologiae,* q. 3, art. 4 of St. Thomas Aquinas, by Benjamin S. Llamzon.

17

God, but subsistent truth." What subsists in God
then is His existence.

I answer that God is not only His own essence, as
was shown, but also His own existence. This can be
shown in many ways. First, anything in a being that
is not included in its essence must be caused either
by the intrinsic principles of its essence or by some
extrinsic principle. An instance of the former is the
proper accidents which accompany a species, as the
power to laugh is proper to man and is caused by
the intrinsic principles of the species. An instance
of the latter is heat in water as caused by fire. Thus,
if the very existence of a thing be other than its essence, then it must be caused either by an extrinsic
principle, or by that thing's own essential principles.
Now it is impossible for existence to be caused only
by the essential principles of a being, since no being
whose existence is caused is sufficient of itself to cause
its own existence. It follows that a being whose existence is other than its own essence has that existence
as caused by another. Now this cannot be said of God
since we say that God is the first efficient cause. It is
impossible, therefore, that in God existence is other
than His essence. Second, existence is the actuality of
every form or nature, for goodness and humanity are
understood as actual only when they are understood
as existing. Existence itself then must be compared
to an essence which is other, as act to potency. But

since in God there is no potentiality, as was shown above, it follows that in Him essence is not other than His own existence. His essence, therefore, is His existence. Third, just as something which has fire but is not fire itself is on fire through participation, so, a being which has existence but is not existence itself is a being through participation. Now God, as was shown, is His own essence. Therefore, if He is not His own existence, He will not be essential but participated being. In that case, He will not be first being—which is absurd. Therefore, God is His own existence and not merely His own essence.

The answer to the first reason is that a being to which no addition is made may be understood in two ways. One, it may be of a thing's very nature that an addition could not come to it. For instance, it is of the very nature of an irrational animal that it be without reason. Two, it may be proper to a certain intelligibility not to require addition. For instance, animal-in-general does not include reason, since it is not within the intelligibility of animal-in-general to have reason; but neither does its intelligibility preclude reason. The divine existence then is without addition in the first way, whereas existence as a common term is without addition in the second way.

The answer to the second reason is that existence can have two meanings. One, it can mean the act of existing. Two, it can mean the composition of a *proposition which the mind forms when attaching a predicate to a subject. Taking existence in the first meaning, we cannot know the existence of God as we cannot know His essence. Only in the second meaning of existence can we know God, for we know that the proposition which we form about God when we say "God exists" is true. This we know from His effects, as was shown above.*

THE COMMENTARY

THEOLOGIANS hold this article's conclusion certain on the basis of faith. Their textual proof is Exodus 3: "I am Who Am, and He Who *IS* sent me to you." In this text, God, by saying that HE IS, signifies his substance; otherwise, creatures also *are,* and God would not have given any unique and proper characterization of himself in saying I AM. Compared to Him, creatures are said not to be, v.g., Isaias 40: "All the nations are as nothing, thus are they before Him." The Holy Fathers unanimously affirm this conclusion, and in the text cited in the preceding article, the Master of the Sentences refers to their pronouncements.[1] If this conclusion were not true, it would follow that the divine essence is not infinite simply and absolutely, for the divine essence would not then intrinsically include existence itself, which is the greatest perfection. See St. Thomas' many other demonstrations of this point in *Contra Gentes,* 1, c. 22-23.

Now someone may say: if this is a conclusion of faith, how is it demonstrated? The same question can be raised about all of the conclusions of the preceding and the following articles, and thus one and the same answer will apply to them all. We do not understand those conclusions of faith as belonging immediately to faith. Rather we take them as belonging to faith in the same way as the conclusion "God exists" is said to belong to faith, even though it is demonstrated, for if such a conclusion is denied, a clear denial of a truth which belongs to faith immediately follows. Conclusions of this kind are thus said to belong to faith. A denial of them would indicate that the authority of the Scriptures is not infallible, and that an article of faith is not true, for one who denies the existence of God would deny all the articles of faith. We say the same thing with regard to the other divine attributes which are demonstrated by natural reason. If they are denied, God's existence, which is the basis of our entire faith, would be denied.

*   *   *

This article contains a subtle and metaphysical position, very different, as Cajetan says, from that of modern writers[2] who think that essence and existence are identified, not only in God, but in every being. This is why I want to examine and clarify this matter carefully.

*   *   *

Before proceeding, we have to look at a few points in order to understand St. Thomas' reasons and position in this article.

Notice in his first reason how he says that proper accidents are caused by the principles of the species. One correctly asks by what kind of causality they are said to be caused by such principles. The answer is that we are talking here about a certain kind of efficient cause from which there is a certain simple emanation of effects, but through the one act by which it produces a substance, not through another act effecting a new change. Examples of this would be the light of the sun, which is caused by the essential principles of the sun's substance, and the cold which comes from the substance of water. This cold may be impeded, but, once the impediment is removed, the cold comes forth immediately. This is said to be from the generative principle of water. Again, a stone is said to have a sort of efficient cause of its natural motion, since by a certain simple emanation it straightway follows a downward motion when impediments are removed.[3] In the same way proper accidents and powers of the soul emanate from the soul itself.

Secondly, notice the proposition St. Thomas holds in his first reason, namely, that no being is sufficient to be a cause of its own being, as long as it has a caused existence. One wonders why this is so, since man, for instance, has the power to laugh, which is a caused power. However, man sufficiently accounts for his power of laughter by himself, since the very definition of man shows that he is indeed able to laugh. Thus, there is no contradiction in saying that a being has an efficient cause of its esse and yet is the sufficient cause of its own existence through its own essential principles. This is precisely where the difficult and mysterious problem we are about to examine begins, namely, with the existence and essence of creatures. Meanwhile, it should be pointed out that there is quite a difference between properties in relation to their essential principles in a species, and these same essential principles in relation to the act of existing itself.[4] For a property, v.g. risibility, already presupposes an actual essence, and, thus, it emanates as an accident, which is a being of a being. On the other hand, esse itself, since it is formally[5] that by which essence is, cannot possibly presuppose essence as the cause from which it flows since this would imply the prior existence of that same essence—a clear contradiction. For instance, since a thing is formally white by whiteness, it would be a contradiction to suppose a thing white even before it had whiteness. In the same way it is altogether unintelligible how anything which has a caused existence can be a sufficient cause of its own existence.

Now one could perhaps ask why, according to our reasoning, a being with a caused existence can in no way be a sufficient cause of its own existence, whereas

St. Thomas seems to imply in the article that indeed esse is somehow caused by a being's essential principles. The answer is that essential principles are a material cause of esse since they themselves can receive the act of existing through which they are first actuated. Indeed, these essential principles are understood only to the extent that they are ordered to esse, just as transparency is a cause of light in the sense that it makes the reception of light possible. And although esse itself, as received in an essence composed of essential principles, is specified by them, still it (esse) receives no perfection from such a specification. Rather esse is constricted and brought down to being of a certain kind, for existence as a man or as an angel is not absolute and unqualified perfection. Now this is exactly what St. Thomas has often insistently proclaimed, although Thomists will not listen: namely, that esse is the actuality of every form or nature.

Look at the second reason given in this article. Here he says that esse is not received in a subject as a recipient and as something perfectible, but rather as that which is received and is perfecting that in which it is received. Insofar as esse itself is received, it is contracted and, if I may so put it, "imperfected." We shall say more on these points later.

There is also a problem regarding how precisely this second reason should be understood, for St.

Thomas says that goodness and humanity are not referred to as actual unless they are precisely existing. This seems to be false since, when I know a rose and name it, I refer to its actuality without signifying that it is existing, as, for instance, when I say that a rose is a very lovely flower, etc.

To this difficulty, one could answer from Cajetan's teaching on St. Thomas' second reason, namely, that any quiddity or nature, no matter how actual in the line of quiddity, still is potential in relation to esse, for wisdom and goodness are taken as actual precisely when taken as existing, and so too with humanity, equinity, etc. Hence, esse is the actuality of every form, and no nature is said to be completely actualized until it is actually exercising existence. So far this is Cajetan's position. Now, this solution appears to be less than satisfactory, for the way we understand a thing through a proper concept is also the way we express that thing.[6] Now we understand quite clearly the nature of a triangle, even though it may not exist actually, and so we express quite clearly the nature of a triangle. Cajetan's comment on St. Thomas' statement that goodness or humanity is not understood as actual unless signified precisely as existing is that existence should be understood as the last actuality. This does not seem to be the correct way to put it; for esse is the first act of any being, not the last. Clearly this is so, since being is what is first understood and in this is included esse, or an intrinsic order to esse as to the first act. Thus, it seems to me that, when St. Thomas says that no form is signified as actual unless we signify it as being, we must understand him to mean form in relation to esse, for this is the way we understand form, whether that being exists actually or potentially. This position is based on being as the object of the intellect.[7] * However, I admit that when a thing is understood as actually existing it has a greater perfection than when it is understood as in potency. For the rest, the quiddity of things other than God says nothing about their actuality or non-actuality. Thus abstractly understood, the quiddity can be perfectly defined.

Cajetan points to a textual difficulty about the second argument. The answer seems to involve two contradictions. If, after demonstration, we affirm that this proposition, "God exists," is true, then we know it is objectively true that God exists. Now this is to know God's esse. So, we know not only that the proposition "God exists" is true, but we also know the act of existing as belonging to God Himself, especially since a proposition is said to be true or false depending on whether the thing it talks about *is* or *is not*.[8]

---

* An asterisk indicates that translations of pertinent passages from other works by Banez are given in that note.

See Cajetan's *2 Post.* c. 1, on this difficulty. He has a brief and good answer, however, in his commentary on this article.[9] He points out that this is the difference between God's esse and the esse of other beings, namely, that God's esse is identically God's very substance, *quod quid est,* for the proposition "God exists" is in the first mode of direct predication.[10] The esse of other beings, by contrast, is found differently, namely, by distinguishing from their quiddities. This is the basis for the other difference, namely, that the esse of God is, strictly speaking, the precise object of the question: what is He. Only indirectly is He the object of the question: IS He; namely, insofar as He is the basis for the truth of the proposition. Now the esse of other beings does not in any way relate to this question "what is it," but simply and objectively to the question "is it." Thus, when we know that any of these other beings is, we not only know the esse which indicates the truth of the proposition, but we also know the very existence of that being since it is known precisely as it is knowable. It is otherwise with God. When we know that He is, we are said to know the actual truth of the proposition, not the absolute esse of God as it is knowable, namely, as of His very essence. This latter we know only indirectly, insofar as it suffices to ground the truth of this proposition: God exists. Thus, in the proposition "God exists," our knowledge attains not only the truth of the proposition, but also the existence itself of God insofar as it relates to the truth of the proposition.

One can press the point of these demonstrations even further, for through proofs not only do we reach the esse of God insofar as it relates to the truth of the proposition "God exists," but we also know that it is of the very essence of God, and that God is subsistent esse Himself. The preceding answer would thus be false. The answer is that, although we come to know this truth through rational proofs, namely, that esse belongs to the very essence of God and that He is subsistent esse Himself, and infinite, immutable, eternal, and many other attributes, which are of His very essence, we nevertheless know all these vaguely and through a certain negation or analogy to creatures. We do not know them through a proper concept which expresses His quiddity just as it is. This is what St. Thomas wants to bring out in this solution to the second argument. In other beings we can know the essence itself, even though we may not know their actual existence, since this latter is extrinsic to their essence. But we cannot have a distinct knowledge of God's quiddity unless we explicitly and distinctly know the subsistent esse of God Himself. This sort of knowledge cannot be drawn out of our knowledge of creatures, no matter how distinct our knowledge is. Let what has been said about essence and existence as they pertain to God suffice at this point. Now, in order to understand how it is true only of God that esse is His essence and how every creature is related as something potential to the act of existing, I think it is worthwhile to examine closely what the act of existing is in creatures. To which things and how does it relate? What is its cause? These points are often employed in theological discussions, yet few take the trouble to clarify them.

First question: what is existence?

To begin, let us look at the word "existence." Existence is that by which a thing is understood precisely as actually existing outside its causes. Perhaps too we can say that existence means *ex-sistens,* that is, an actuality "outside" potentiality. Our question here is not about this or that particular existence, but in general about the existence of a creature. What precisely is its intelligibility? On this point there are various opinions.

* * *

One opinion is that existence is nothing but a certain kind of accident received in creatures by which they stand outside nothingness.[11]

The *first reason* for saying this is that existence

is neither the matter nor form of a natural being, nor is it the whole composite. Therefore, it is an accident. The premise is clear enough and is found in St. Thomas. The conclusion is proved in that substance is either matter or form or the composite from both. If then existence is not any one of these, it is not substance.

Secondly, existence informs and actualizes the whole essence of the substance to which it is referred. Thus, it is entirely distinct from substance, just as act is distinct from potency. If then it is neither substance nor something substantial, it will be an accident. Besides, whatever comes to a thing already constituted of matter and form is an accident. Should it be said that it is the act of substance without being received in substance, this would seem to be nonsense. How can a substance exist through an existence which is not within it? Also, if that were true, there could be no reason why Peter exists through this rather than that other existence through which Paul exists, since neither existence is received in Peter.

Thirdly, existence is not distinct from the duration of a being, just as motion is not distinct from time, which is the measure of motion. Now the duration of a being is an accident pertaining to the predicament of quantity or to the predicament *when.* Thus, existence too is an accident. Furthermore, duration seems to be nothing more than the continuation of esse.

Now a being's continued existence is not distinct from itself. Again, the durations of things are distinguished according to the diverse modes of existence. For instance, an *aevum* is the duration of an existence intrinsically unchangeable, though extrinsically changeable; time is the duration of a being intrinsically changeable both successively and continuously; eternity is said to be the measure of a being altogether unchangeable, whose existence is His essence.[12] Thus, existence and duration are identical and belong to the same predicament.

The other opinion is that of Capreolus commenting on S.T., I, d. 8, q. 1, a. 1, concl. 3[13] (and of Gerard commenting on the same question, a. 3, ad 3 against the first conclusion), who holds that existence is the actuality and the form, as it were, of every created thing by which everything is said formally to exist. He says that existence in itself is neither a substance nor an accident, yet that the existence of substance is reduced to the predicament of substance and the existence of an accident is reduced to the predicament of accident. According to Capreolus then, existence does not belong directly to any predicament. In his *De Ente et Essentia,* c. 5, q. 11, ad 8, Cajetan too says that the existence of a substance is a substance, and the existence of an accident is an accident. He says that the existence of a substance is reduced to the genus of a substance as the last formal principle of that substance, since a being is put in the genus of substance because it is capable of being substantial.

To come now to a **decision** on this question.

Let this be our *first conclusion:* existence in its precise intelligibility cannot be an accident, for the precise intelligibility of existence is that of a pure perfection. As such, it cannot be an accident, for no accident, no matter how perfect, is in its intelligibility a pure perfection. Furthermore, existence is found formally in God, and thus it cannot formally be an accident.

Second conclusion. Created existence, the existence of a created thing, does not as such signify an accident. First, the intelligibility of an accident presupposes a being in which it inheres. But to really exist, the existence of a substance does not presuppose a being already actual. Thus, it is not an accident. The major premise is clear since an accident is a being of a being. The proof of the minor premise is that substance itself cannot be understood as existing before it has existence. Thus, existence does not come to an existing substance but rather is that by which substance precisely exists. Furthermore, the very substance itself, whether created or creatable, is not intelligible without an intrinsic and transcendental order to esse or existence. Hence, existence cannot be an accident, for a substance in its own intelligibility does not depend on an accident. Since a substance is understood as a being, namely, insofar as it has or is apt to have esse in itself (and not in another), it cannot then be understood without an intrinsic order to the act of existing itself, for this act, while not a quiddity of substance (hence, substance is seen precisely as created), is nevertheless that by reason of which substance is understood as a being in itself. The final proof is that, if esse itself were an accident, then all the predicaments would be accidents. This is so since the predicaments are distinguished through the diverse modes of being. Thus, if esse itself were an accident, every mode of being would be an accident.

The *third conclusion.* The act of existing is something real and intrinsic to the existent, for esse is that by which a thing is constituted as outside nothingness. Now, I do not understand esse to be intrinsic to the existent in such a way as to be a part of it or its essence, or as though it were something essential (we shall take this point up in the next section), but I do say that esse is intrinsic to the existent insofar as that thing is not said to exist by an extrinsic denomination as, for instance, when place is predicated of it. Esse is said of a thing as something within it though received from another, as personality[14] or even accidents are said to be intrinsic to substance; whiteness, for instance, is said to be intrinsic to some body. Existence is the first actuality, by which a thing is posited outside nothingness, and therefore it has to be within the thing. It is unintelligible how a thing could be constituted as outside nothingness by something which is not internal to it. Furthermore, if the first actuality of a thing were extrinsic to it, then no other actuality could be intrinsic to it. The first actuality is the root of every other actuality. Now since all the other actualities constrict the act of existing itself to some mode or kind of existing, this implies that the other actualities are intrinsic to the existent, while esse remains extrinsic. Finally, were esse not intrinsic to a thing, then in that existent it would be unreceived. That thing then would be self-existing and infinite like the divine existence.

Fourth conclusion. The general consideration of the intelligibility proper to esse, though it involves being intrinsic to an existing being, does not require that it be received as in a subject. This is clear since, otherwise, existence would not formally belong to God. The fact is that it is most intrinsic to Him since it is His quiddity. A parallel to this would be the way we understand wisdom in its own formal intelligibility as not requiring reception in a subject. Such a reception means an imperfection in wisdom, and this is true of created wisdom, not because it is wisdom formally, but because it is created and participated.

Fifth conclusion. The intelligibility of created existence consists more and chiefly in this, that it is a termination which fulfills the potency of substance to become real and to be outside nothingness, rather than in that existence itself be received in the substance as in a limiting subject. For this point there is theological proof. According to the more probable opinion and that of St. Thomas, the humanity in Christ our Lord does not have an existence that is created and received in a subject; rather it exists outside nothingness through the existence of the divine word, which terminates and completes the order of that humanity to actuality. Thus, we understand the formal, direct and proper intelligibility of esse as that by which a being exists outside nothingness. Beyond this, the reception and limitation of esse in a being is really a case of existence as material and imperfect, for if this latter belonged to the formal intelligibility of esse, a creature's existence could not be substituted for by divine existence without this latter being limited by the former. For instance, God would be unable through His own existence, instead of through whiteness, to make something white exist. Hence, the preceding conclusion holds. An excellent illustration confirms the point, for the reason why theologians (and we too will hold this later on in q. 12, a. 2) say that the divine essence can function in place of an intelligible species lies in its unifying function between object and power. The fact that in us intelligible species are accidents inhering in the intellect is due to our intellect's own imperfection. So also, we say here that the proper and formal intelligibility of existence does not include any dependence upon that which through it exists, but consists only in this, that it thoroughly actualizes the order of substance or essence to being and away from nothingness.

Sixth conclusion. Existence which fulfills the potentiality of substance, not only so it is outside nothingness, but also so that substance may exist in itself (not in a subject), is reduced as such to the predicament of substance, not as potentiality nor as proper difference, but as first act, completing the intrinsic mode of substance which exists in itself; that is to say, it is that by which substance primarily exists in itself. Now if I may put this more accurately, the act of existing itself is above all of the categories and is not reduced to any of the categories as to something more noble than esse itself. Rather, this reduction to a category is more a limitation of existence and an imperfection than an entrance into something more perfect. In this reduction the parts of substance are assigned to the category of substance as to something better, which also is the case when differences are set beside a predicament. However, existence realizes genus, difference, and everything in the predicaments. Therefore, in my judgment, it is incorrect to say that esse is reduced to a predicament; rather it is participated in and limited by all of the predicaments. Esse itself does not participate in any of the predicaments but is participated in by all of them, as St. Thomas teaches often, especially in *Quaestio Unica De Anima* a. 6, ad 2.[15] A confirmation of this is that no one would claim that being is reduced to a predicament. We say rather that finite being is divided into predicaments through diverse modes, by which it is limited as a principle internal to every genus and every predicamental difference. Since being means that which has esse, as a potency which has its act, how can one hold consistently that the potency itself is not reduced to a predicament while the act itself is thus reduced? These are points which require extremely refined, not slipshod, metaphysical inquiry.

From here then we proceed to the *last conclusion*. The existence of an accident, by a natural proportion, belongs to an accident, just as the existence of a substance belongs to substance. We go along on this point with the generally accepted opinion, which may also be seen in St. Thomas and which Cajetan explains very well in q. 28, a. 2, ad 2,[16] namely, that the in-existence of any accidental form is really distinguished from the essence of an accident and the esse of the subject. To me, however, it does not seem improbable that the same existence of the substance which directly actualizes substance also actualizes the accidental form.[17] This is a good conclusion since the reality of an accidental form is to the esse of an accident as the esse of a substance is to substance. Hence, the existence of an accident belongs directly to an accident even as the existence of substance belongs to substance.

We now **counter** the arguments for the first opinion [p. 30 above]. The consequence in the *first argument* is denied. An accident presupposes the esse of substance in its intelligibility in order that it may be truly said to be a being in a being. As for the proof of the consequence, it is conceded that existence is neither matter nor substantial form nor the substantial composite. It is the first actuality, completing and terminating the intrinsic mode of substance. Thus, it is reduced in some way, as we said, to substance, not as participating substance, but as something directly participated in by it.

In the *second argument* the antecedent and main consequent are admitted, but what follows is denied, namely, that, since it is neither substance nor something substantial, esse is therefore an accident. This is an incorrect conclusion, for existence itself, according to its proper intelligibility, even in created things, is neither a substance nor an accident. It is the first actuality and realization of substance or accident. The well-known saying that there is no third between substance and accident is true if it is understood correctly. It is true that there will be no being, that is, something that has esse, which will be neither substance nor accident. So, esse itself or existence is not the being which has esse but is that by which or through order to which something has esse. Thus, we should not wonder that existence itself is neither substance nor a part of substance, nor an accident nor of the essence of an accident. For the rest, by an improper meaning of "reduction," we admit that sometimes it is reduced to substance, sometimes to accident, depending on whether it actuates a substance or an accident.

Every time an addition comes to a thing constituted through matter and form, that addition is understood to come to a being in act, either according to actuality or according to reason. Thus, esse is presupposed either according to actuality or according to reason. But prior to existence, either according to actuality or according to reason, there exists nothing and nothing is understood, since being is the object of the intellect. Hence, existence is never understood to be superadded to a being already composed of matter and form, for such a composite, if it excludes an order to existence, is nothing.

What has been said in the third, fourth, fifth and sixth conclusions also holds for the retort.

Now for the answer to the *third argument*.[18] First, I reject the minor, for to perdure is intrinsically and formally to remain in existence, a kind of an absolute. This does not entail a relation to anything extrinsic. Even though it may be explained and known through order to time, this order still does not belong to its formal intelligibility, for esse is prior in the natural order, and so it is more fundamental for a thing to remain in its own existence than for it, while so perduring, to be in time. Similarly, the having of a quantitative mode of being is more basic to a thing than its being localized.

Secondly, I deny the major, for, over and above existence, duration adds permanence and continuation. Hence, to exist by the clock is not simply to exist, that is to say, simply and absolutely, for this latter is nothing more than to have existence actually outside one's causes. Existence in a measure of time, or duration, is not included in the absolute meaning of existence. Hence, existence is absolutely distinguished from the duration of a thing, and this also contains the answer to the confirmation given above. Though the continuation of a thing and the thing itself are not distinguished as one thing from another, still they are distinguished as a thing and its mode.

The answer to the last confirmation is that it proves only that duration has a certain dependence on the existence of a thing, not that it is formally identical with esse.

With regard to the opinion of Capreolus and Cajetan [p. 32], two remarks have to be made. First, how are both of them to be understood when they say that esse or existence is reduced to substance insofar as it actuates substance? For this reduction, as we said, is not that of an imperfect to a more perfect thing, but rather that of the most perfect actuality, the very act of existing in itself, to the best receptive potency.

The other point is that they call esse the ultimate actuality of a thing. This requires an explanation. Esse or existence is the first actuality, not only as regards the goal of the one generating, but also in its formal intelligibility, since nothing is understood unless it either has esse or an intrinsic order to esse. Thus, it seems false to say that esse itself is the end intended by the one generating and hence is the ultimate actuality of a thing. This point is confirmed in that in the process of generation, while a man is generated, there can be no embryo prior to its own existence. The very fact that we say "it is an embryo" shows we already understand existence. Indeed, something potential cannot be understood unless it be already understood that esse itself can actualize that potency. Hence, I am dissatisfied with Cajetan's explanation of the above point, namely, that existence is called the ultimate actuality of a thing because generation ends with it. Certainly this business of calling esse ultimate actuality is rarely found in St. Thomas. In the *Quaestio Unica De Anima* a. 6, ad 2, you will find that he says that esse itself is the last act, which can be participated in by all. In this very place, however, if you continue reading, you will see how esse is called last act, namely, as the supreme, most excellent act, which indeed perfects all other acts, for every other form relates to esse as potency to act. Perhaps to be more acceptable we can say that esse is the first and last actuality of any being: first in the order of intellectual composition, last however in the order of intellectual resolution. For instance, when the intellect relates its idea of being, which is its proper object, down to man, what it understands is first to be in itself, which indicates substance, then to be body, to be living, to be rational. In all these steps esse itself is seen as first act. Now if one wishes resolutively to retrace his steps upward to what is simpler, he will arrive at esse itself. Beyond this he cannot go. This shows how esse itself is first and last act. In the last analysis it is so purely and simply a perfection that no composition whatever can be found in it, although all things except God are composed of esse and essence as of act and potency. Our discourse up to this point then has been on the intelligibility of esse itself.

Second question: the distinction between esse and essence in created things, namely, whether esse is distinguished from essence.

Let us first consider the arguments for the **negative side.**

If esse is really distinct from essence, it follows that God can separate esse from essence, and conserve both, for, when two things are really distinct, nothing can make it impossible for God to conserve one without the other. Here the falsity of the consequent is immediately evident, for, if essence is conserved and exists and on the other hand we suppose that God separates esse from essence, we end in two contradictories: it does and does not have esse. By a similar reason, St. Thomas says, in q. 66, a. 1, that matter cannot be without form or else matter would exist actually without act, which is impossible.

Secondly, if esse is really distinct from essence, it follows that it would be pure act and thus would be God, for if esse is really distinct from essence, it is an act which does not include any potentiality. Thus, it is pure act. The antecedent is proved in that esse itself has no potency whatever, unless such a potency comes from esse being identified with essence; otherwise, if esse itself were to be composed of act and potency, there would be an infinite series.

Thirdly, if esse is really distinct from essence, it

follows that it exists by itself, for the act of existing, since it includes no potency, cannot exist through another act. Thus, it exists through itself. This, however, is true of God alone.

Fourthly, if esse is really distinct from essence, it follows that immaterial substances are composed of esse and essence. The consequent is false, therefore. The proof here is that whatever includes distinct things is a composite of them. The minor's proof is that it is impossible for an *unum per se* to result from two components, unless one of these components relates to the other as potency to its act, for from two actually existing things we do not get an *unum per se,* as Aristotle teaches in his second book of *De Anima* and the seventh book of the *Metaphysics,* text 49. Now in immaterial substances, clearly the esse cannot be the potency; nor can the essence, since this will then either be absolute or only relative potency. Now it cannot be absolute potency, since this would make it pure potency as prime matter; nor can it be relative potency, since what is relatively a potency, simply has to be actual. In that case the essence of an angel, apart from esse and precisely as distinct from esse, would simply be in actuality.

Fifthly, if there is a real distinction between esse and essence, it follows that the distinction obtains between two fundamentally real things. Now this consequent is false; therefore. . . . The proof of this is that a real distinction is a real relation which necessarily exists between two extremes which really exist. The minor is proved in that essence, as distinct from existence, is not objectively actual and hence cannot be one extreme of the real distinction from existence, the other extreme.

Sixthly, if esse is really distinct from essence, it follows that in composite material things there is a two-fold real substantial composition, one of matter and form, another of esse and essence. Consequently the resulting composite would only be an *unum per accidens*.

Now, in this article St. Thomas explicitly teaches **the opposite** of all the preceding conclusions. He holds that God alone is His esse.

There are three main positions on this difficult point.

The *first position* asserts that esse and essence are by no means objectively distinguished in such a way. Rather, they are distinguished only conceptually with, however, a foundation in things. This sort of distinction is customarily called a reasoned mental distinction. Herveus holds this position in his *Quodlibetales* 7, q. 9, and Gabriel in his 3, d. 6, q. 2, Aureolus in Capreolus' I, d. 8, q. 1, and Durandus in I, *Sent.* d. 8, first part of the distinction, q. 2; as do all the nominalists. They hold that essence and esse are not any more different than race and running.[19]

The *second position*[20] is held by Scotus in 3 *Sent.,* d. 6, q. 1, and Alexander of Hales in 7 *Metaph.,* text 22, and Agostino Nifo in 4 *Metaph.,* disputation 5. Master Soto also follows this opinion in 2 *Physics,* q. 2. These doctors say that existence and essence are distinct, not only mentally, but really formally, or "formally by the very nature of the thing," not as one thing from another thing, as Soto says in the text cited above. There are indeed strong reasons for this position, since by this procedure the authors of this position seem able to answer satisfactorily arguments against the extreme positions.

The *third position*[21] holds that essence is distinct from esse as one thing from another thing, such that not only is the proposition "essence is esse" false formally, but also the proposition "essence is a thing which is esse." Capreolus[21] holds this position in I, Dist. 8, q. 1, Cajetan in his brief work *De Ente et Essentia,* c. 5, q. 10, Ferrara in *Cont. Gent.,* 2, c. 52, Soncinas in 4 *Metaph.* q. 12, Iavellus in his treatise on the transcendentals, c. 4, and it seems to be the opinion of St. Hilary in Bk. 6 of his *De Trinitate,* the place St. Thomas cites in his *sed contra.*

To **decide** now on the truth of the matter.

Let this stand as our *first conclusion:* essence and

esse are not only distinct mentally. This position seems common to writers of noteworthy seriousness, both in philosophy and theology. In his brief work *De Ente et Essentia,* c. 5, and in *Cont. Gent.,* 2, c. 52 and 53, St. Thomas holds this position. This conclusion is proved from Sacred Scriptures and the holy Fathers in the places already mentioned and in the preceding article. They attribute to God as proper and unique to Himself and His essence and esse are distinguished only mentally. Hence, the same should not be said of created things. Secondly, this is proved in that the proposition "essence is esse in created things" is generally rejected by all theologians and philosophers and seems to be inadmissible, for it is unique to the divine essence that in a formal sense esse is predicated of it. Now if created esse is distinct from its essence only mentally, doubtless the same proposition would be true of it, just as divine essence, though mentally distinct from, *is* His own esse. Thirdly, from the opposite position, it would follow that existence belongs essentially to creatures, so that "man exists" would be an essential proposition. The consequent is false, therefore. . . . For that proposition is not an eternal truth, since before the creation of the world it was false. This is so, for no instance can be cited where some real act is identified really and formally with some thing without belonging and being intrinsic to that thing. Reason proves this, for, if the formal intelligibility of one thing is identical with the formal intelligibility of another thing, it is impossible for those two not to have an intrinsic and essential connection, hence, etc. Finally, this is proved in that, if essence is really identical with esse, it is hard to understand how the divine Word assumed humanity without a created existence, communicating to that humanity directly, not merely its personality, but also divine existence. St. Thomas holds this position explicitly in *S.T.* III, q. 17, a. 2, where he proves that in Christ our Lord there is only one esse, the divine existence.

Let this then stand as our *second conclusion:* it is much more probable and more in accord with Theology, to hold esse as really distinct from essence as one thing from another. This seems to be St. Thomas' position in the places cited above. The proof of this is that the constitutive mode of a supposit is really distinct from that supposit as one thing from another, as was said in the preceding article. All the more distinct then is esse from essence,[22] * for esse does not come to essence except through supposital-ity. Esse itself is the proper act of the supposit, as St. Thomas teaches in II, q. 17, a. 2. Also, the constitutive mode of the supposit is more intrinsic to that supposit than esse, for that mode is in the defini-tion of a supposit, while esse is not: only an intrinsic order to esse is in every being. Secondly, esse is received from an efficient cause and depends upon it for both becoming and conservation, while essence belongs directly and properly to the creature without dependence on an efficient cause, for it is eternally true that to be a man is compatible with Peter. But that Peter exists is due to the efficient cause. Thus, esse cannot be the same thing as essence. Thirdly, a true potency and a true act are really distinct just like matter and form. Now essence is a true potency with respect to the act of existing. Therefore, the two are really distinct as one thing from another. Fourthly, if the esse of a creature were the same thing as its essence, it would follow that esse is not really received in essence, for the same thing is not received into itself. Now if esse indeed were not received in essence, it would be unlimited and infinite simply, even as God Himself, for esse cannot be limited by some other act, as we saw in the preceding section. Against Durandus,[23] the point is quite effectively proven in I *Sent.*, d. 8, that essence is at least really and formally distinct from esse. This is confirmed, since divine essence is precisely infinite because it is really and formally His esse. Thus, if the essence of a creature were its own esse, it would not have a limited esse, nor indeed a received existence. Finally, this conclusion is proved in that, if we may so put it, we understand the mystery of the Incarnation better, since the humanity is drawn not only to the personality of the Word, but also to His existence, according to the more probable opinion. It would be awkward to maintain that the humanity of Christ is actualized by divine esse and by another created esse.

At any rate, let this be our *last conclusion:* Scotus' opinion and that[24] of Master Soto, cited in the second place above, which differ little from the position we have just explained, can be held with probability. The arguments against it by those who hold the third opinion can be answered by this illustration. Figure actuates quantity and terminates it, and quantity is related as a potency to figure, yet figure and quantity are not really distinct as one thing from another, but formally from the nature of a thing, or really formally as they say; or, they are distinct as thing and mode of a thing, as, when one bends a rod, it does not seem that he has produced anything really distinct from the rod's quantity, but rather that he has effected the mode of the quantity. However, we are following St. Thomas' position as Capreolus and Cajetan understand it.

Here then are our answers to the arguments presented above [p. 44].

We **counter** the *first argument* by denying the inference. By proceeding that way you could prove that prime matter can exist without form and that a vital activity can exist without a vital principle, which are contradictions. We say then that even though these two principles are distinct as one thing from another, since one of them has an intrinsic order of dependence on the other for its existence, that one cannot be conserved without this other. Since essence as existing depends on received esse, it is a contradiction to maintain that it exists without existence.

We answer the *second argument* by denying the inference. The answer to the proof presented is that esse itself, although it is really distinct from essence, is nevertheless limited in that it is received in essence. Hence, it is not pure act. The imperfection of potentiality, however, does not belong to esse by reason of itself but because it can be received. And in this it differs from uncreated esse, which is not distinguished from essence.

We answer the *third argument* by rejecting the inference for the same reasons.

We answer the *fourth argument* by admitting the inference but denying the minor. The major premise in the proof is admitted, the minor denied. Essence in immaterial things, except God, is as potency in relation to esse. Now, is this relative or pure potency? The answer is that the essence of a substance is not pure potency in the way that prime matter is pure potency in relation to substantial form. Nevertheless, the essence itself of a thing is absolute potency in relation to the act of existing. Nor is it unintelligible that this same essence should at the same time have its own specific formality intrinsically, since it has this in virtue of its intrinsic order to esse as to its first and last actuality. As St. Thomas says in the *Quaestio Unica de Anima,* art. 6, ad 3, there is nothing to prevent one form from relating to another form as potency ordered to its act. Diaphaneity, for instance, with regard to light is potency to its proper act and yet that diaphaneity itself is the form of the diaphanous body. In the same way, the essence of an angel, even though it is a subsistent form, still is absolute potency in relation to esse, even though it has its own formality, by means of which it determines esse itself in a more perfect way than material things.

The answer to the proof in the *fifth argument* is that the essence itself is an actual part of the thing but is actuated through existence, which is really distinct from it, in the same way that matter and form are really distinct and that between them there is a real relation.

As for the *sixth argument,* I concede the inference, but I deny that it is unacceptable to posit in material things one physical composition of matter and form, and another composition, a metaphysical one, of esse and essence. Nor is the result of this an accidental unity, since what results from the physical composition of matter and form is the potential principle in the metaphysical composition of essence and esse, since esse itself actuates the entire substance composed of matter and form. Thus, there is a great difference between these two compositions. The first is one of intrinsic and essential parts, while the other is a composite of the entire essence and a principle other than essence, which actuates it and comes precisely as the actualization from nothingness of that whole creatable essence. Thus, esse is not a part of essence but is received in essence.

Third question: whether existence is more perfect than the essence to which the existence belongs.

The *first argument* for **the negative side** is that a man is more perfect in that he is a rational animal than in that he exists; thus, the essence of man is more perfect than his existence. The consequence is clear, and the antecedent is proved in that for a man to be rational is an intrinsic, necessary, and eternal thing, while for a man to exist is something contingent, hence. . . .

Secondly, the existence of a stone is univocally the same as the existence of a man. Their difference is in the most perfect intelligibility of man manifested in the differentiating notes of sensible, living, and rational. Therefore, esse itself is not more perfect than the specific essence of man.

Thirdly, to live and to understand are greater perfections than to exist, for they add something over and above esse. Hence, in man esse is not the greatest perfection.

This is confirmed in that among principles, what is more general and more determinable is the more imperfect. Now esse is the most general and most determinable of all principles, for it is determined by all the other perfections: by life, wisdom, etc.

This is confirmed secondly in that, as St. Thomas teaches in *De Veritate*, q. 7, a. 6, ad 7, that which is the more general by way of predication is the more imperfect. Now esse is what is most general by way of predication. Hence, it is the most imperfect.

Fourthly, esse is more or less perfect on account of greater or less perfection of the essence in which it is received. For instance, esse is more perfect when received in the essence of a man than when received in the essence of a horse. Therefore, the essence itself is more perfect than esse. This is proved by the Aristotelian maxim that in causation the source of the greater perfection is also the greater of the causes involved.

Fifthly, the essence of each thing is directly and through itself placed in the predicaments. Esse, however, is placed there only indirectly and reductively, through the essence in which it is received. Hence, essence is more perfect.

Sixthly, existence is compared to essence as this

latter's termination, like a point to a line. Now the point is not more perfect than the line. Thus, existence is not more perfect than essence.

Seventhly, that is more perfect in man in which he is made to the image and likeness of God. But man is made to the image and likeness of God in that he is intellectual, endowed with free choice, capable of happiness—all of which pertain to man by reason of his specific essence. Hence, this is the most perfect of all the principles in man.

Eighthly, Christ our Lord assumed a most perfect human nature without assuming the existence of that nature. Hence, existence does not belong to the perfection of human nature, and it is a mistake to say that it is more perfect than the essence of man.

Finally, it is argued that the first effect of substantial form is the specific essence itself, while esse is only its secondary effect. Hence, the specific essence is more formal and perfect.

*   *   *

On this question Scotus in 4 *Sent.* d. 1, q. 1, teaches that esse is the most imperfect of all the perfections.[25] This opinion is followed by Soncinas in 4 *Metaph.,* q. 13, and by Ferrara in *Cont. Gent.,* 1, c. 28.

Other modern Thomists, however, are attempting some sort of **middle position** by maintaining that, absolutely speaking, esse is the most imperfect of all the principles but that in a certain respect it exceeds all other perfections, namely, in that it is the first actuality of all the other perfections, since other perfections are outside nothingness through esse. They point to St. Thomas in *Cont. Gent.,* 1, c. 28, as supporting their position.

*   *   *

To come now to a **decision** on this question.

Let this be our *first conclusion:* absolutely speaking, esse is a perfection greater than the essence to which the esse belongs. This is proved first by the authority of St. Dionysius[26] in *De Div. Nom.,* c. 5, where he asserts that of all the perfections we have received from God esse is the greatest. So also, Aristotle in 8 *Ethics,* c. 11, says that the greatest benefit given us by God is that we *are.* St. Thomas also in I, q. 4, a. 1, ad 3, says esse is the most perfect principle of all. Here he is explicitly talking of the actual existence of creatures. Secondly, this is proved in that esse is the actuality of all the perfections and of all the forms. It is compared to essence as act to potency. This is a most frequent teaching in St. Thomas. See especially *S.T.* q. 4 of the first part, a. 1, ad 3, where he explicitly says that esse itself is the most perfect of all and that it is compared to all the others as act, and that it is not compared to the others as a receiving principle to what is received, but rather as a received to a receiving principle. Hence, it receives no perfection by being composed with essence. Also see St. Thomas in *De Verit.,* q. 8, a. 4. Thirdly, this is proved in that, as long as essence does not have esse, it does not exist simply but is only potential. Now when it has esse, it is, without qualification, an existent. Hence, esse is more perfect than essence. Fourthly, this is proved in that in God Himself what we understand most of all is not that He is life, wisdom, or power, but that He is subsistent esse itself. In that are understood all the other perfections, since it is unreceived esse, hence, unlimited. Therefore, esse is not perfected by being received in essence. This is so since its precise reality is thus constricted and limited. The most perfect cause is the proper cause of the most perfect effect. Now the esse of creatures is the most proper effect of God, since they are from non-being. Therefore, that effect is most perfect. This is confirmed in that all beings desire existence most of all. Hence, it is the highest good of all.

Second conclusion. Relatively speaking, the essence which received esse may be said to be more perfect insofar as it limits esse to a determinate species. This conclusion can be proved by the arguments given above for the opposite position. But this conclusion is relative indeed, since truly it is better for esse to be unreceived and unlimited, for, were it not received in an essence, it would contain all the formal perfections of everything. Thus, just as form is simply not perfected by being received into matter, so also esse acquires no perfection upon reception into essence. It is true, however, that, on the supposition that esse is to be received and limited, it is somehow perfected by reception into a more rather than a less perfect essence. In this case, we should strictly speak of esse as less constricted, and, if I may so put it, we should talk of esse being rendered less imperfect by reception into a living rather than non-living essence or into an angel rather than a man.

With these remarks for a background, we can now answer the arguments above (p. 54).

We **counter** the *first argument* by saying that no perfection belongs to man, not even animal rationality, unless it is understood as an intrinsic order to existence, as potency to act. Hence, I deny the antecedent, for, by the very fact that we say a man exists, we understand that rational animality is perfected by existence, not that existence is perfected by rationality.

The answer to the proof of the antecedent is that all that necessary and eternal truth is predicated of man as it is found in God, not as something created.[27] * Now, however, we are comparing a created essence with a created existence, and we say that esse itself is more perfect since it is what accounts for essence being outside nothingness; for, before a man exists, he is actually nothing in himself but *is* only in his cause as in an effective and exemplary principle.

To the *second argument* the answer is that, although according to the generic intelligibility of substance a stone exists equally as a man, still the esse itself of a man is much more perfect than the esse of a stone, not because it is perfected by the essence of a man but because it is less constricted by the essence of a man than by the essence of a stone.

To the *third argument,* the answer is that, if to live and to understand did not include esse, they would not be greater perfections than esse, but, since they include and receive esse itself, they are greater perfections than the esse which lacks life and intelligence. They would not be greater perfections than esse if this latter had not been received. As for the first confirming statement, the answer is that what is more common and determinable is more imperfect when commonness and indetermination are understood as matter and potency, which receive some other principle. Now esse itself is most common in the formal order. It is not determinable as a principle that receives something, but as that which is received in everything. Hence, the consequence is invalid. It should be pointed out, secondly, with St. Thomas in *De Verit.,* q. 20, a. 2, ad 3, and with

Dionysius c. 5 of *Div. Nom.*, that, if to live and to be are considered separately so that one is not included in the intelligibility of the other, then esse is a greater perfection than to live. But, if to live includes esse, then it is not surprising that to live should be a greater perfection than esse which is received in a non-living being. As for the second confirming statement, the answer is that something common, according to predication, which is determinable as potency to act, is imperfect. We have stressed, however, that esse itself is not determined as potency by act.

To the *fourth argument* the answer is that esse is more or less perfect according to the greater or lesser perfection of the essence in which it is received, not as though this is due to a formal cause, but because of the more or less imperfect material principle. This is as if you were to say that gold is more or less perfect on account of the greater or lesser mixture of it with another metal, for it would be most perfect and purest if it were unmixed with any other metal. As for the Aristotelian axiom, the answer is that for it to apply validly both extremes of the causal series must be positive beings, and further that, because one extreme is such a kind of being, the other should be the same kind. This is irrelevant to our discussion here, for it is a fallacious understanding of causality to say that esse is perfect and essence is perfect, and that, because essence is perfect, esse itself also is perfect. Indeed, esse is not perfected by essence except relatively in the sense explained in the second conclusion.

To the *fifth argument* the answer is clear from what we have said in the preceding question. There in the sixth conclusion we said that the reduction of esse itself which actuates substance to the predicament of substance is not as what is imperfect to what is perfect, but as actuality to potency.

To the *sixth argument* the answer is that existence is not compared to essence as the point of a line to the rest of the whole line, but as the point realizes the line without being a part of the line. For the rest, existence so realizes essence that it is more perfect in the intelligibility of being, while the point is not more perfect in the intelligibility of quantity.

Regarding the *seventh argument,* the fact is that what is most perfect in man is that in which he is made to the image of God. But pray tell, how does this come about except that esse is less limited when received in a rational than in a bestial nature? Otherwise, there simply would not be any man! So we deny the consequence of the argument because, in comparing essence to esse, it does not properly grasp the relation and distinction between the two.

To the *eighth argument* the major and minor premises are conceded. However, I distinguish the consequence where the inference is made that existence does not belong to the perfection of human nature. I say that, as regards the quidditative perfection, I grant the consequence. But in the sense of first, direct and completive perfection of human nature, by which it is formally constituted outside nothingness, I deny the consequence. The human nature of Christ our Lord had this sort of perfection from a source other than the existence proper to itself, since the human nature in Christ our Lord was drawn to the existence of the infinite Word, which substituted for the proper esse as an actualizing principle. Here the intelligibility involved is a very precise one, as we observed in the first question.

We shall take the *last argument* up in the next question. Meanwhile, I deny altogether that actual esse is a formal effect, whether primary or secondary, of the substantial form as though it could flow out from itself into itself. Rather, every form is compared to esse as diaphaneity to light. We will explain this at length in what follows.

Fourth question: whether all actual existence in creatures is caused by God.

Because this is an extremely difficult question, it is best to look into the various opinions of doctors who take opposing positions on the matter. But be-

fore everything else, we should note that we are talking here about the esse of beings which can be generated and corrupted. The esse of beings that cannot be generated and corrupted such as the esse of an
angel, the esse of the rational soul, the esse of the
heavens, is produced by God alone, a position wholly
based on faith. Moreover, we also wish to explain
here the dependence of esse on particular causes, and
on the form of the supposit to which esse belongs.
Philosophers hold opposing positions on this point.
Some hold that particular causes directly cause esse
in the effect while denying this of the form in the
effect. Others say the opposite, namely, that esse
emanates from the form as from an efficient and formal cause, though not from secondary causes. In
order then to come to a conclusion on this question,
we should investigate every cause on which esse depends.

*   *   *

The *first argument* for the **opposing position,**
namely, that actual existence is not the effect of God
alone, is from St. Thomas, who attributes such causality very often to creatures as in *De Pot.,* q. 7, a. 2.
In the body of the article he says that every cause is
alike in that it causes esse. Also in *S.T.,* I, q. 42, a.
1, ad 1, he says that the first effect of form is esse,
as in q. 50, a. 5, and q. 90. a. 2, ad 1; *De Verit.,*

q. 21, a. 4, ad 6. In these places he contends that esse follows form. There is a special text in *Cont. Gent.,* 2, c. 54, where he says that just as light is related to what is lighted, and whiteness to a white thing, so also is form to esse.

Others too are accustomed to argue from St. Thomas *S.T.,* I, q. 3, a. 4, in the body of the article, where he says that it is impossible for esse to be caused only by the essential principles of a thing. In commenting on that exclusive phrase, they take St. Thomas to mean that esse somehow is caused by the form, that esse is caused by the intrinsic principles and by some other principle.

The *second argument* is based on reason. When a horse produces a horse, it really generates the other; hence, it produces its esse effectively. The antecedent is clear. The consequence is proved in that to generate is to give esse. The common definition of generation given by Aristotle and other authors is that it is a change by which the existence of a thing is acquired in an apt subject. Indeed, every one admits that the formal term of generation is the existence of a thing. This is confirmed in that a horse effectively gives the horse it generates life and sensation. Thus, it also effectively causes its existence, for one who effectively causes the lower grades of being, say, life and sensation, also causes the superior grades such as being. Perhaps you will say that all this argument really shows is that a horse in generating another horse produces a "this being" since it produces this living, this sensing being, and that from this argument it does not follow that it also produces existence. But the opposite is true, for being formally says esse. So, if one effectively gives the grade of being, he also effectively produces esse, just as one who effectively causes a living thing effectively causes life.

The *third argument*. Creatures conserve the esse of other creatures together with God; hence, they also effect esse itself. For the certainty of the antecedent, see St. Thomas, *S.T.*, I, q. 104, a. 1, ad 2. The consequence is proved in that not more is required for production than for conservation. In fact, St. Thomas often insists that the action by which a being is conserved and that by which it is created are the same, and that conservation of esse is to be attributed to the producer of esse.

The *fourth argument*. A particular cause is constituted as an agent precisely through existence. Hence, he produces the same existence in the effect. The antecedent is proved in that an efficient cause operates according to whether it is in act, as is clear from Aristotle and the philosophers. Now a cause is in act formally through existence, for the essence of a cause is compared to existence as potency to ultimate act. This consequence is proved in that the principle of operation in a cause is its act and form. An agent produces something similar to itself. Hence, if it is an agent insofar as it is in act through existence, then it produces an effect insofar as the effect itself is existing. Consequently, it also produces esse.

The *fifth argument*. The grade of existence is prior to the other grades of being which are found in the produced effect. Hence, a particular cause first reaches esse. The antecedent is clear, since the grade of existence is prior and more common. But that which is more universal and common is prior. The proof of the consequence is that a cause cannot reach a lower grade without first reaching a higher grade, especially when there is an essential subordination among the grades of being.

The *sixth argument* is based specifically on form as the principle of existing. It is axiomatic among almost all metaphysicians that existence is a secondary effect of form. The theologians admit this, maintaining that God can supply a substitute for form in causing existence. This they hold as a fact in the mystery of the Incarnation. Indeed, they assert that, if Christ had relinquished his humanity, esse would have come immediately from the natural proper form. Hence, esse is an effect of form.

The *seventh argument*. Existence is a substantial act of the supposit, and hence is caused by a form of the supposit. The proof of the consequence is that what is substantial to a thing should not be held as altogether extrinsic to it. Therefore, existence either is form or is caused by the intrinsic principles of a thing. This is confirmed in that otherwise it would follow that accidents, which are caused by form either mediately or immediately, are more intrinsic and are more closely conjoined to a supposit than substantial existence—an absurd conclusion. Nevertheless, these thinkers maintain that esse comes from without.

The *eighth argument*. "An angel exists" is a necessary and direct proposition. Hypothetically, it is demonstrable. Hence, existence is related to a subsistent form, as obtains in an angel, as an emanating intrinsic property. The proof of the consequence is that to be intrinsically connected with form is to flow from that form. This is confirmed in St. Thomas, *S.T.,* I, q. 54, a. 2, ad 2, where he says that the essence of an angel is the entire basis for its being.

The *ninth argument*. It is argued that, if esse were not from form, it would follow that the existence of accidents would not be caused by the essence of a subject, but would instead be immediately produced by God. The consequent is false, therefore. . . . This conclusion holds; for the same reason that you use to hold that God causes substantial existence by Himself alone, we will use as our reason for saying that the existence of accidents is produced by

God alone. The proof of the minor premise above is that it would follow, in the case in question, that the esse of accidents did not depend directly on substance, nor would it have an intrinsic dependence on the essence of a supposit. This conclusion is proved by the fact that existence is directly produced by God alone, as is substantial esse; hence, by its very nature it depends on God alone.

Finally, it is argued and proved that esse is not from God alone. If it were, it would follow that existence is created, and this consequent is false. The minor premise is clear, for it seems unreasonable that in every production, present and future, God produces something entirely new. This conclusion is clear in that all created things are immediately produced by God alone.

* * *

Concerning this question, Scotus, in 4, d., q. 1, holds that particular causes produce the existence of things directly. This opposes St. Thomas, who holds that existence is the effect of God only. On this point fairly recent authors[28] follow Scotus.

Among Thomists, however, Ferrara[29] in *Cont. Gent.,* 2, c. 21, holds that there is only one difference between God and secondary causes in the production of esse. God, simply and directly, causes the existence of things, whereas creatures cause esse not simply, but determinatively. In c. 54 he says that existence is the formal effect of form, a point he elaborates in c. 55.

Capreolus,[30] in I, d. 8, q. 1, ad 3, in commenting on the arguments of Henry and Gerard against the first conclusion, holds that existence is solely from the form since form is what makes the subject capable of existing. And Gerard agrees with him.

*   *   *

To **decide** on the truth of this matter.

Let this be the *first conclusion:* Particular causes give esse directly to their effects, each one in its own way. For instance, fire in generating fire makes fire exist, and a heater produces the existence of something hot. This conclusion is first proved by the authority of both the philosophers and the theologians, who very often presuppose this conclusion as a first principle. Secondly, this is proved by reason. A particular cause educes the effect from potency into act simply; therefore, it gives esse and actuality to the effect, for to cause simply is to move to actual existence what was in potency. This is confirmed since corruptive causes, for example, fire corrupting the air, are said to destroy directly the particular existence of the supposit which existed previously, insofar as that existence was the act of the supposit. For instance, the cause which destroys Peter also causes Peter's existence to cease, even though the same esse that was in Peter remains in his soul. Hence, generating causes are said to give esse directly to that which is generated.[31] * Thirdly, this is proved in that particular causes, as every one in this discussion agrees, effect the composition of esse and essence in the supposit; hence, they produce the effect's existence simply. The consequence is maintained since a cause is said to cause the being-such of the effect simply either when it produces the form through which a thing is, as when a horse generates a horse, or when it effects the composition of form with its subject, as when someone unites something already white to a wall, thereby whitening this latter directly. Thus, when particular causes join existence, which is the form of being, to the essences of supposits, they are said to give esse to the produced things simply. Besides, it seems absurd to deny that my father gave me existence. The second argument given above towards the beginning of this question proves this conclusion sufficiently.

Second conclusion. We must add that creatures do not cause existence simply, nor as principal causes in their effects. This is proved first by the fact that every creature presupposes esse in its operation. Hence, it does not cause esse directly. The antecedent is clear. No creature can operate from non-being. Besides, every creature presupposes the subject which it contacts physically. On this point see Aristotle and authors in 1 *De Generatione,* textual commentary 11, and St. Thomas, *S.T.,* I, q. 45, last article and last reply, and q. 44, a. 1. You may say that this merely proves that the creature does not produce that esse which it presupposes, but that it corrupts this esse and thus produces the esse which follows in the generated effect. I hold the opposite, for production is a direct and absolute causation in which something not-such is made such. A white thing is not produced from something white, but from a non-white. When a man generates a man, he produces from something not-man; hence, it is a direct production. See Aristotle on this point in the text cited above, and in 5 *Physics,* textual commentaries 6 and 7, and wherever authors treat of the kinds of motion. In our present discussion, in order for creatures rightly to be called causes of existence directly and absolutely, they should produce existence from non-existence, which is impossible. This will become clear in our last conclusion.

Now if you use our first conclusion above to argue that creatures give and directly produce the esse of a whole thing, hence causing existence directly, the consequence is denied. From the previous statements, one can see that saying creatures give esse does not necessarily mean that they produce the form of existing. In the production of a man, for instance, the one generating gives esse to the man generated even though he does not produce his soul.

Third conclusion. Particular causes do not produce existence, strictly speaking, as instruments. Here we oppose those who, while agreeing with us in the second conclusion, maintain that God impresses upon creatures a certain transient power so that they may produce the existence of their effects; that is, existence is communicated from God through them. The conclusion still holds, however, since this power is used at the creature's discretion. Besides, it is absurd to say that in causing an effect a particular cause is both principal and instrumental cause as regards the same effect, that in the effect produced something is directly caused by the secondary cause, and then that something is caused by him as assumed by God.

Fourth conclusion. Particular causes effectively cause the determination of esse. Observe carefully now that existence involves two things. First, it is the act of a being absolutely. Thus understood, it involves no limitation. Accordingly, insofar as existence belongs to the supposit in which it is received and insofar as it is already produced and limited, this limitation comes to existence because of its reception by a particular essence. As St. Thomas teaches, what is received has limitation from the receiving subject. We say, therefore, in this conclusion that a particular agent concurs as a particular effective cause of this limitation. The first proof of this is that this limitation is not from God alone; hence, it is from a particular efficient cause. Now clearly this efficient cause is not the essence which receives the esse. Hence, it will be the cause producing the supposit. Moreover, the causal agent disposes the supposit to become apt to receive existence. Therefore, it effectively determines the supposit to exist, for whatever particularity the supposit has in the order of existence is from the causal agent. That very principle by which the supposit is made apt for existence is determinative of it. Therefore, what efficiently causes that disposition also determines the esse of that supposit effectively. Many texts in St. Thomas should be interpreted in the light of this conclusion, for often he talks of creatures as not causing being, but this being. For instance, see his *De Potentia,* q. 3, a. 1, in the body of the article, where he says that every being has an act determined to one genus and to one species; hence, none of them is productive of being as being, but rather of being as determinate being in this or that species. His reason is that the agent's effect is similar to the agent itself. Thus, a natural agent does not produce being directly but determines a pre-existing being to this or that kind of being; for instance, to fire or to whiteness or to something of this sort. Furthermore, he says, God produces esse while creatures determine esse. In other places you find him saying that creatures produce this particular esse. This is all to be understood and explained as the limitation we explained in our conclusion, through which the effect is this being with a determinate and limited esse. So much regarding active causation of esse.

Fifth conclusion. No created form is a cause, whether efficient, formal, or final, of esse. Let us prove the parts of this conclusion separately. First of all, no form is an efficient cause of esse. An efficient cause operates, insofar as it is in act, through existence; hence, if a form produces something, it produces that, insofar as it is actuated, through esse. The antecedent is certain and is presupposed as a principle by Aristotle. A cause not actuated by existence is merely in potency, and hence it cannot give act to the effect unless it actually has the effected perfection. This is confirmed since otherwise potency, precisely as potency, would reduce itself to act, which is against what Aristotle has in 3 and 8 *Physics* and in 12 *Metaphysics.* This conclusion is proved in that here the form is taken as efficiently causing, by itself, its own esse before it is even existing. Besides, existence belongs directly to the whole composite and is communicated to the parts. Hence, it does not come effectively from form. The antecedent is certain. We will talk about this at length in 1 *De Generatione,* God willing. We now prove the consequence by

showing that otherwise form would cause itself,
which is absurd. This concluson holds, for, if form
caused its own existence effectively, it would make itself exist and reduce itself from potency to act; it
would cause itself. See other reasons in St. Thomas,
Cont. Gent., 1, c. 22, and *De Ente et Essentia,* c. 5,
towards the end. Now, that esse is not a formal cause
is proved in this way. Form is related to existence as
potency to act, as receiver to the received. This is
not formal causality. Furthermore, every act of existence is the actuality of every form and is, therefore,
the form of all forms, and not the reverse. In addition, it is impossible to explain just how and under
what aspect essence informs or actuates existence.
Finally, it would follow that the form of being is
not the very act of its existing or order to that act,
which is false. For that is the form of being which
completely realizes and constitutes the thing. If therefore essence is related to esse as the form of esse,
essence will be actuating; it will be basically what
constitutes that existent as an existent; it will be
what actuates and completely realizes it, and essence
would then be the basic act of being.

Now you may argue that form specifies esse and
hence relates to esse as a kind of formal cause. The
antecedent is seen in that human esse is distinguished
from the specific esse of a horse through the form of
man, which differs in species from the form of a

horse. The answer is that esse formally and intrinsically takes its specification from its transcendental order as act to a given form. Only extrinsically, as a termination and as a receiving subject, does form specify esse. For the rest, within this context, the intelligibility of form is closer to that of matter, just as the form of the heavens is said to be specified by the matter in which it is made, and artifacts are said to be specified by their subjects. Now for the proof of the third part of the conclusion, namely, that form is not a final cause of existence. Existence is the direct termination of form, not the reverse; thus, existence is the end of form rather than the reverse.[32] * Secondly, existence is the fundamental perfection of a thing; hence, form is ordered to it as to an end. The proof of the antecedent is that each thing is called good and perfect insofar as it is existent. Thus, Aristotle in *Ethics,* 10, c. 7 and 8, c. 11, says that existence itself is what is most loveable and desirable in all things. The truth of this statement will appear in q. 6 below. Now that form is a material cause of existence is clear from what has been said, since it is receptive and limiting of existence itself. Just as matter in relation to form is understood as a material cause because it receives and determines form, so also matter, as well as form, as also the supposit, is a material cause of existence.

The *sixth conclusion.* Here we should add that

form, in the order of formal causality, determines matter towards the reception of existence. This is proved in that form gives the first act to matter; hence, form is understood precisely as disposing matter to receive the act of existence. This is proved, secondly, in that this limitation and proportioning of the subject, which is necessary for the reception of existence, requires some real intrinsic form. This can only be the form of the supposit, therefore. . . . Notice, however, that form is said to be the formal dispositive cause for existence, not indeed as an immediate cause, but nevertheless as a principal cause. For, besides form, we also posit suppositality, by which the supposit is capable proximately and immediately of this existence.

The *final conclusion*. Existence is the proper effect of God alone. This is St. Thomas' conclusion in this first part, q. 8, a. 1 in the body of the article, and q. 45, a. 5, and *Cont. Gent.* 2, c. 21, and 3, c. 66 and very often in other places of this latter work. Among Thomists, no one would doubt that this is St. Thomas' conclusion, but the doctors are not sure exactly what he meant by this conclusion. Cajetan, in texts on this part cited above, says St. Thomas means that esse is the direct effect which immediately depends on God alone. It does not follow from this that creatures do not produce esse as secondary causes. Ferrara also talks in this manner in his commentary on *Cont. Gent.* 2, c. 21, and 3. Other Thomists interpret St. Thomas to mean that existence is the formal and adequate object of God alone, since God alone is the cause of each participated esse and of whatever pertains to the esse of a thing. This cannot be said of any creature. Others, however, say that St. Thomas means that God, alone and without any limitation, produces existence and being precisely as being. For our part we prefer to take St. Thomas' words just as they stand, instead of following any of the above opinions or producing a new commentary, for the three opinions given above do not explain the meaning of St. Thomas, who everywhere and consistently attributes this effect as properly belonging to God and proves it with most profound reasons. He would not have failed to give profound reasons if he had meant any of the three opinions cited above, for all those meanings are admitted by all without dispute. That is not the problem. What we maintain is that no cause produces esse efficiently except God Himself.

This conclusion is first proved by using St. Thomas' reasons. God alone is essentially His own esse. Creatures have participated esse. Thus, God alone produces esse.

To appreciate the force of this reason, notice that to have something through participation can happen in two ways. First, one shares something from another. In this way whatever is in a creature comes to it as a participation from God, for all that we are, we are from the Lord. In this sense then it is sound to hold that what is essential to a thing is also participated from another. However, St. Thomas' way of concluding does not follow this line. Second, something is said to be participated because it does not belong to a subject but is wholly extrinsic, coming from a producer and conserver, as light in a diaphanous material.

Secondly, notice that the power to cause presupposes the nature and essence of a thing. A being is such a being in itself before it is productive of a perfection similar to itself in another. Now every being is said to be such and such a nature by reason of its own form and whatever directly pertains to itself. Consequently, it is said to be properly causative of what is similar to itself by reason of its own form and nature, v.g., by its own essence water exists as water. That it can cause something similar to itself and can cool, belongs to it directly because of its own form. On the other hand, just as by itself it is not hot, so also by itself it does not have the power to heat. It can heat as an instrument of what is hot in itself.

These observations bring out the force in St. Thomas' arguments. No creature, by itself and by its own nature, has esse; rather, this is communicated and conserved by God. Hence, no creature by itself is a cause of existence, whether in general or in particular. That causality is from God alone. The antecedent is fairly certain and should be held on the basis of both faith and philosophy. The consequence is proved in that the power to cause existence presupposes the act of existence itself in the acting cause. However, if the esse of the cause itself enters and is communicated from without, then the cause does not of itself have the operative power to cause existence unless you wish to say that it possesses that power as an instrument, which we have already refuted. Thus, God alone, whose existence is of His very essence, has the power to produce and conserve that same act of existing in creatures. The second proof of the conclusion is that every creature presupposes in its own activity something produced by God alone and, hence, presupposes its existence. The antecedent is proved in that every creature produces out of something; hence, it presupposes that something, something produced by God alone. This is confirmed since otherwise there would be no cogent reason for denying that the power to create can be communicated to creatures, for, if these causes presupposed nothing in their operations that was dependent on God alone, then they would be able to produce out of nothingness. Thirdly, we want to demonstrate this point and to explain the preceding reason at greater length.

Prime matter is both incorruptible and ingenerable, conserved by God alone. Hence, God alone gives the existence communicated to prime matter. The antecedent is certain. The consequence is proved in that it is unintelligible how matter is not generated or how it is conserved by God alone, if He Himself did not give it existence. If particular causes effected the existence of matter, they too would be the ones who produced and indeed conserved it. Now you may object that according to this position, prime matter too, in relation to God, corrupts and is produced anew. This is answered by denying the conclusion. The effect of the divine action is the act of existence, which is never absent from matter. Particular causes determine this esse in the processes of change. Hence, the argument retains its force if particular causes produce this and destroy that previous existence. We see this further in the fact that we cannot explain by any other reason how God is the cause of the whole being, unless He alone causes the esse both of the form and matter and of the whole. If creatures effected this same thing, then they would be said to be the cause of the whole thing. St. Thomas never asserts this. Thus, we skip other reasons which can easily find throughout St. Thomas. Summarizing, we say that particular causes only dispose and determine the subject in order that it may be apt to receive esse through the form. It is God who causes

esse from without. There is a handy enough illustration of this in St. Thomas when he talks of the
essence and esse of creatures. He compares essence
to a diaphanous material and existence to light which
actuates the diaphanous, for instance, air. The light
does not emanate from the essence or diaphaneity
of the air, but the diaphanous matter is in potency,
by reason of diaphaneity, to the reception of light.
Now, when a natural agent, operating in sunlight
that illumines the air, corrupts that air and from it
generates water, which at the very same instant of
its generation is illumined by the same sun which
illumined the air, no one will say that that natural
agent by its own action produced the light, nor that
by itself it existed as the cause of lighting. We say
rather that that light depends on the sun as a kind of
efficient cause both for becoming and for continuance
in being. Yet the particular light which was in the air
ceased to *be* upon the corruption of the singular
subject, and another particular light began to exist
in the particular water generated. The particularity
and individuation of the water produced is due to
the natural efficient agent; thus, this agent was re-
sponsible for the light of the sun being produced in
this numerically singular subject. In this way esse
begins and ceases by the action of a particular agent
on another which it corrupts and generates, for it is
certain that the esse of the generated being is not

the same esse that was formerly in the being that was corrupted. Neither can it be said that the agent which generated the new being generated its esse or effected it, any more than it can be said that in the example the natural agent produced the light in the lighted water. However, it is true that the generator of this singular substance is consequently the efficient cause of the determination of its esse so that it is precisely this esse received in this subject. I must say I do not understand how this doctrine is misunderstood by so many, even among the most learned who profess to follow St. Thomas. In St. Thomas there are many clear texts of this point, and the understanding of existence itself demands it. For instance, in *S.T.,* I, q. 4, a. 1, ad 3, St. Thomas teaches that esse itself is the most perfect of all principles. He says the same thing more explicitly in *De Potentia,* q. 7, a. 2, ad 9, where he takes esse as the act of all other principles. For no being has actuality except insofar as it exists. Hence, esse itself is the actuality of all things and also of all forms. He says, thus, that it is not related to other principles as recipient to what is received, but as the received to the receiver. This is what St. Thomas maintains. In my judgment, it is very clearly stated that God alone can be the efficient cause of esse and the source of existence itself. Were esse understood as flowing out of some form of the thing as from a formal principle, as to be white flows from whiteness or to have the power to laugh flows from rationality as its source, then it would not suffice to say that esse itself is the first actuality of all things, even of forms. Indeed, that from which esse itself flows, whether as a kind of formal or originating cause, would have to be already understood as having an actuality which is not dependent on esse in the line of formal cause since here existence itself would supposedly flow from it as from a formal or originating principle. Now what they say, namely, that actual existence is the secondary effect of substantial form, implies a contradiction of the principle that existence is the first actuality of all things and of all forms. To understand some other effect as the primary and formal effect and existence as the secondary effect of substantial form is no longer to take existence as the first actuality of all things and of all forms. This implies that substantial form is seen to have a certain formal effect without being understood as previously actuated by the first actuality, which is existence. If those who think differently on this point weighed these arguments carefully, perhaps they would render to Caesar what is Caesar's and to God what is God's. For God, who is the First Being, whose essence is Unreceived and Unlimited Existence itself, is the sole efficient cause of all acts of existing, which are received and which are limited by that in which they are received as by a material cause, though in another order the recipient of esse may be substantial form in relation to matter or the composite. Unless one blinds himself, he can see this clearly illustrated in the case of a rational soul. When a man is generated, we realize that everything requisite for the generation of a singular substance is at hand, not less but more than what is requisite for the generation of a horse. We admit also that in the generation of Peter the form is not educed from the potency of matter. This is only necessary when the term of the generation is less perfect. Thus, in the generation of Peter, the very form is not from any efficient cause but God, who creates that soul from nothing. The esse of this substance comes from God alone and is received in the soul as in a subject. The esse does not flow from the soul but is the soul's first actuality. Therefore, when John generates Peter, he cannot be said to be the efficient cause of the esse which is in Peter, not even with respect to Peter's singularity, for the esse of this singular soul is communicated to it through its creation from nothing. It is not good thinking then to say, as our opponents do, that, because fire generates fire, it is the cause of the fire's esse. Nor is it wise to say that the one who generates Peter is an efficient cause of Peter's existence and that, therefore, the one who generates Peter causes Peter's existence. This alone is true: that the generator efficiently disposes the matter for the union of the soul with the body. The existence of Peter is accomplished then through the esse of the soul, which is communicated to the matter and the supposit. There is no necessity for positing the generator as the cause of the esse. On this basis it will be fairly easy to answer the arguments of those holding the opposite position.

To **counter** the *first argument* [p. 64], which is drawn from texts in St. Thomas, we can cite opposing texts in St. Thomas in which he maintains much more clearly that esse itself is the proper effect of God alone. For instance, he explicitly says in *De Potentia,* q. 7, a. 2, that esse must have some cause superior to everything else, by whose power everything is caused to be, and that His, the first cause's, proper effect is esse. And here in *S.T.,* I, q. 8, a. 1, in showing how God is within every being, he says that created esse is His proper effect, which He causes in things not only when they begin to exist, but also as long as they are conserved in existence. In a similar way, light is caused in the air by the sun as long as the air remains illumined. And since esse is what is most intimate to every being and the deepest principle of every being, since it is a formal principle in relation to all else which is found in a being, it follows that God is in all things intimately. See also q. 45, a. 5, where he explicitly stresses the same point and *Cont. Gent.,* 3, c. 66, where he teaches the same.

There is one answer to all of the texts which have been cited to support the opposite position. Whenever St. Thomas says that to cause esse is common to all efficient causes, he should be understood to mean that they cause esse only insofar as they determine esse to the supposit or the nature. This is what he says in the fifth reason of *Cont. Gent.*, 3, c. 66: all beings other than God effect esse by particularizing and determining the action of the first agent, that is to say, the effect of the first agent. They cause as their proper effect, he says, other perfections which determine esse. Regarding those particular texts in which esse is said to follow form and the argument that just as light is related to what is lighted so also form is related to esse, the answer is also from St. Thomas in *Cont. Gent.*, 2, c. 54. There he says that, even to the very form itself, esse is act. It is clear then how esse itself follows form, for it follows in the way that act follows the final receptive state of a subject. Even though form itself in the line of essence is a formal principle, with respect to existence it is still in the line of potency and is receptive of that by which the supposit exists. In the same place St. Thomas explains this very well when he says that it is on this basis that, in beings composed of matter and form, form is said to be the principle of being, for it is the completion of substance, whose act is esse itself. He cites as an example the diaphanous quality of air, which is a principle of illumination because it makes for the proper reception of light. From this doctrine it is easy to understand what he had said a little while before. In that chapter St. Thomas meant to show that only a substance has esse as *that which is,* that the composition of matter and form is not the same as that which is, and that the composition of matter and form is not the same as that of substance and esse. Hence, in the third argument he shows that the form is neither esse itself, nor does it have esse as that which is. Rather, esse is that by which the substance *is.* The relation here, he says, is that of light to being lit and of whiteness to being white. Just as whiteness is not a white thing, nor light a thing lit, the substantial form is not the esse itself by which something *is.* However, he immediately explains a very great difference, for to be lit or to be white is not the act of light itself, that is, as actuating light, or whiteness itself. On the other hand, the esse itself actuates the substantial form. This is his position. Hence, we see that even to the form itself esse relates as act. It is for this reason that, in beings composed of matter and form, esse is said to be the principle of being, just as the diaphanous material is the principle of lighting in the air, namely, because it is the realization of substance, whose act is esse itself. Thus, when you read in St. Thomas that form is that by which something is, read the preceding texts and you will understand the sense in which form is the cause of existing. That sense is certainly the same as the sense in which diaphaneity is said to be the cause of light, because it is that by which the body lighted receives the light.

The solution to the *second argument* can be easily seen from what was said. We concede that, when a horse generates a horse, he effectively brings a horse into existence. He also effectively determines esse itself to the esse of a horse. However, I will never agree that the efficiency of a particular cause reaches the act of existing absolutely; rather the cause effectively determines it to this kind and limits it to this individual in the way that a subject limits materially. For the rest, God Himself through His efficiency effects all being insofar as esse itself, which actuates and perfects everything, is His own proper effect.

The consequence in the confirming statement is denied. The answer to the proof is that, when a higher grade is essentially contained in a lower, perhaps it will be true that whoever effectively causes the lower grade also causes the higher grade. But esse itself, as we often said, is not contained in any quidditative grade of a creature. Regarding the other points, the solution suggested here is a good one. The answer to the further reply is that being, in its essential predication, formally means order to esse.

Clearly then, it is not necessary that whoever produces this being in the singular should produce his existence. He who generates Peter, although he effects this being, still does not cause his existence.

The answer to the *third argument* is that no creature conserves the esse of another creature, absolutely speaking, but only insofar as it conserves the determination and limitation of the act of existing itself. The influences of the heavens, for instance, conserve man in being and life by conserving the environment necessary for the body and the individual. In regard to the texts quoted from St. Thomas to support the argument, we answer that we can cite nothing more favorable to our position than what St. Thomas teaches in that article. If Thomists read it carefully, they would not disagree with us, for, among other things, St. Thomas teaches there that every creature is related to God in the way that the air is related to the illuminating sun. Since that light is not rooted in air, it ceases instantly upon the cessation of the sun's action. So also, he says, every creature is a participated being, and God alone is Being essentially. In the solution to the first objection, he says that esse directly follows the form of a creature. However, this presupposes God's influx, just as light follows the diaphaneity of the air as long as there is the prior influx of the sun. Let those who say that esse flows from form as from its source reflect on this point and see that their teaching is a departure from St. Thomas.

Some say concerning the *fourth argument* that the existence of a particular cause is only a necessary condition for the action of the particular cause. I think they are wrong, for the existence of a particular cause is the first actuality of every form of the agent and is the foundation of every activity of the form. Nevertheless, we must observe that, just as existence itself is received in the forms and limited by them, so also it reaches their effects insofar as existence is limited by those effects, not insofar as existence is simple and without qualification.

The consequence in the *fifth argument* is denied. In fact, the opposite conclusion follows: precisely because the grade of being is first, it ought to be attributed to the first cause. Once there is the influence of this first cause, a particular cause concurs in the determination and particularization of the effect of the first cause to *this* supposit of *this* species.

By now the answer to the *sixth argument* is clear. Those who say the existence of a being is a formal effect, even though a secondary one, should not be considered good metaphysicians. We must insist simply that esse follows form just as light follows diaphaneity; which is a material cause of the former, that is to say, an immediate disposition to receive light.

The answer to the *seventh argument* follows from

what was said in the first question. We deny that existence is the substantial act of the supposit, as though it were from the essence or quiddity of the supposit, but we can say that it is the substantial act, that is, the first principle, which actuates the form of substance. Similarly, light is the act of the diaphanous through its diaphaneity. The conclusion of the confirming statement is denied. Accidents are not caused by the form unless the actuality of existence, which is immediately received in the form even though it does not have its root in the form, is presupposed. However, that existence itself, limited by the form, is the root of such accidents as flow from the existing form.

In answer to the *eighth argument*, it should be denied that the proposition "an angel exists" is, without further qualification, a necessary proposition. It is necessary only according to a physical necessity, based on the supposition that an angel has once been created or produced by God. But one should note that the necessity of "the heavens are," "an angel is," is not obtained immediately and directly from their intrinsic intelligibility as, for instance, "risible" is obtained from the intrinsic intelligibility of man. Otherwise, "an angel is" and "the heavens are" would be eternally true like the proposition "man is risible." They are, however, said to be necessary in the sense that, once they have received esse from

God, they are conserved by Him alone. No other cause in the whole nature of things, extrinsic or intrinsic, could make them cease to exist. Thus, only God, who transcends the whole order of the universe, is able to annihilate such beings. They are freely conserved just as they are freely created.

The answer to the confirming statement, concerning our understanding that the essence itself of an angel is the ground for its whole existence, will be clarified later by St. Thomas.

In the *ninth argument,* the inference is denied. The existence of accidents is not existence simply, but existence in another. Hence, it is not contradictory for it to emanate from a substance already in existence, especially since the existence of accidents follow the specific determination and individuation of the accidents.

In the *last argument,* the inference is denied. Existence is not what has esse, but that by which something *is.* Hence, to be created is true directly only of the existent itself and of that which from nothingness receives esse. And so, whenever after creation something new is produced through the corruption of another, this cannot be said to be created since it is not made from nothing. Nevertheless, in every action of a natural agent the action of the creator is presupposed, not indeed as creating something novel, but as conserving things through the continuation of the action by which he gives esse to them. Hence, the proper effect of God is esse itself, absolutely speaking. Look up what St. Thomas says on this point, further on in q. 104, a. 1 and 2, and q. 45, a. 5, and in *De Pot.*, a. 7, where he says that esse itself is the most universal effect, the first and most internal to every other effect. Thus, such an effect properly belongs to God alone as to a proportionate power. What has been said up to this point should suffice for this difficult question.

Fifth question: whether accidents have an existence proper to themselves and really distinct from the existence of substance.

There are several opinions on this point. Scotus answers in the **affirmative** in 4, d. 12, q. 1. Likewise, Soncinas in 7 *Metaph.*, q. 5, conclusion 2, who offers three arguments to prove his point.

This is his *first argument*. No form is ever present in any being without communicating its formal effect to that being, for form and formal effect are inseparable. Now, in Peter there is, for instance, whiteness, whose formal effect is to be white, making him to-be-white. But to-be-white is not to-be-man, for this latter can remain itself without the former.

Therefore, in Peter there is this twofold esse. The same argument can be extended to all the other accidental forms.

This is confirmed since it is true of every form that it gives a certain esse. All forms give a certain esse naturally, not a substantial one, of course, but an accidental one, really distinct from the substance.

This is his *second argument*. There can be no potency without its proper act. Now esse is the proper act of essence. Hence, there can be no essence without its own proper act. But the esse of man is not the proper esse of whiteness nor of some other accident. Therefore, as many accidental essences as there are, there will also be the same number of properly corresponding existences.

This is his *third argument*. In the Eucharist, the accidents of bread exist, but not through the existence of bread, since after consecration nothing of the bread remains. Therefore, the accidents of bread have their own proper existence. Consequently, accidents have their own proper esse distinct from the existence of substance. Dominic of Flanders is of the same opinion in his *Metaph.* 7, q. 1, art. 5.

Now Master Dominic de Soto holds the **opposite opinion** in his I *Physics,* q. 6, in his definition of matter, but he does not prove it, though it can be proved. The *first reason* is that esse belongs to that thing which is undergoing becoming. Now becoming holds only for substances which exist of themselves. By one act, Peter is produced, and all the other accidents requisite for his integrity and perfection are simultaneously co-produced. Hence, esse belongs to them only in this situation. Consequently, they do not have an esse of their own but exist only through the existence of the substance. This is confirmed in that matter is not said to have its own existence, for it is not created by God directly but is rather con-created. Likewise, all accidents which begin their existence with a certain substance are not themselves produced directly but are co-produced in that production of the substance. Indeed, by their very nature some accidents require that they be produced in this manner, as can be seen in the case of proper accidents. Therefore, it must also be said that accidents do not have their own existence.

This is proved *secondly* in the beginning of Aristotle's *Metaph.*, 7, where he says that an accident is itself a being only because it is the "such" of a being, namely of a substance. Hence, it *is* only insofar as it is *something of* a substance, and so does not have its own esse—otherwise, it would be a being, not merely *something of* substance. This is also confirmed, it seems, by what we usually mean when we say that the being of an accident is being-in, that is, it does not have its own esse or proper existence but the existence of its subject. Thus, accidents do not exist except through participation or communication of the subject in which they exist.

Thirdly, if accidents had their own existence, this latter would be an inherence. But this consequent is false, therefore. . . . The inference is valid since every mode of actual being in the objective order is either existence in itself or existence in another. Now accidents do not have existence in themselves; therefore, if they have an esse, this will be "in another." The minor is proved since the existence of an accident is either an aptitudinal or actual inherence. Now it cannot be aptitudinal inherence because this is the *essence* of an accident, as Cajetan proves in *De Ente et Essentia,* c. 7, q. 16. It cannot then be its *existence,* for in every created being existence is distinct from essence. But neither can we admit the second possibility, actual inherence, for the accidents in the Eucharist exist truly, yet not through actual inherence, because whatever actually inheres is unintelligible without an actual subject. The accidents in question do not actually inhere since they have no subject in which to inhere. Rather, those accidents are altogether actually separate from a subject, as St. Thomas teaches in *S.T.,* III, q. 77, a. 1. Therefore, in no way can it be said that inherence is the existence of an accident, at least not if we talk of accidents as really distinct from substance.

Of these two positions I once thought Master

Soto's the more probable one. It did not occur to me then that it was against the mind of St. Thomas. Now, after considering the point carefully, it seems to me that the other position, which holds that the existence of accidents which are really distinct from substance is also really distinct from the existence of substance, is much more probable. It seems to me that St. Thomas explicitly holds this position in III, q. 17, a. 2. There he inquires as to whether in Christ there is only one esse and states that in Christ there is only one esse, which belongs to the supposit as to that which has esse. He states consequently that there is nothing to prevent the multiplication, in Christ or in one supposit, of that esse which belongs to the accidental form, for the esse by which Socrates is white is one esse, and that by which Socrates is musical is another. St. Thomas speaks thus in c. 7 of *De Ente et Essentia* towards the beginning, and in I, d. 3, q. 2, a. 3, and d. 20, q. 1, a. 1, and *Cont. Gent.* 4, c. 14. Cajetan takes this position as exactly that of St. Thomas, below in q. 28, a. 2, and in his commentary on *De Ente et Essentia,* c. 7, where he says that from the composition of whiteness with snow an esse is effected by which both whiteness *is* and the snow is white.

Those who defend the identity of essence and existence all follow the same position, for, just as an accident has an essence distinct from substance, so also does it have an existence distinct from substance. Thus, they talk consistently, even though their premises are false.

And so we shall **assert** and prove from true premises that the existence proper to an accident is distinct from the existence of a substance. We may take as established what was said in the first question, namely, that existence is the act by which precisely every being exists. Now this act is not found equally in all beings, for in some it is so imperfect that it depends on the existence of a subject. In others, however, it is more perfect and communicates existence to the subject. The former way of existing belongs to accidents, the latter to substances. Thus, substance is said to have an existence in itself, while accidents have existence in another. The reason for this can be gathered from the different essences themselves according to which esse is limited to a determinate genus and species. Since there is then the utmost diversity between substance and accident (since substance is directly intended by nature, while accidents are intended as a completion of substance), it is concluded correctly that a substance has esse in itself, while an accident has esse in the substance. With this one can formulate the reason for this position. One and the same act cannot be both dependent and independent of a subject. However, the existence of an accident is by its nature an act dependent on a subject, while the existence of a substance is an independent act. Therefore, the two cannot be identical.

But, you will say, a formal or rational distinction will suffice here. No; it will not.

First that dependence belongs to the act according to its entity and arises from its imperfection. Therefore, it is necessary that the diversity be in the very entity where such a dependence is affirmed and denied. This is confirmed since otherwise, by the same sort of reasoning, it could be said that the same rational soul is really dependent on matter from one aspect and independent according to another aspect, and that on one basis it is mortal, while on another it is immortal.

Secondly, I argue in this way. Its very existence is the basis for saying that an accident formally inheres or in-exists. Therefore, the existence of an accident is formally an existing-in. This conclusion follows since nothing is said to be formally such except on the basis of its form, which is precisely within a being. Thus, the existence of a substance is not formally an existing-in; otherwise, a substance would on this account be formally existing-in. Hence, the existence of an accident is distinguished from the existence of a substance.

Finally, there are many accidents which, of their own intrinsic entity, are of the supernatural order. It is necessary then that they have an esse of the supernatural order. But there is no substance except the divine which is of the supernatural order. Therefore, there is no existence of substance which is the existence of these accidents. The conclusion is proved in that existence is proportioned to the essence and is of the same order.

With this for a background, we can **counter** the arguments of the second position.

The *first argument* [p. 96 above] is answered by denying the minor. As for the proof, I say that, even though in fact many accidents are produced through the same action by which substance is produced (which we will not dispute at the moment), still they can be produced through other actions which terminate in themselves, as quality is produced through alteration and quantity through augmentation. Secondly, the answer is that it does not follow that, just because something is co-produced in the production of another, it does not have an existence distinct from the latter. What follows rather is that what is co-produced is something belonging to this latter. Thus, accidents are of the substance and are produced as the completion and perfection of this latter. As for the confirming statement, the answer is that the reason why matter does not have its own proper existence is not because it is con-created with simple bodies, which were first produced from nothing by

God. On the contrary, it does not follow from the fact that it is created and from the mode of creation that it has its own existence, since it is not directly created. Hence, although, naturally speaking, that which is directly produced has its own existence, it does not follow that, because something is not directly produced, therefore, it does not have its own esse. For instance, if God were to create a man from nothing as regards both soul and body, the soul would then be said to be con-created, since it would be produced as a part of the man and yet would have its own proper existence. Nor would the whole man have any other esse except this one communicated to it, for the soul's esse is the person's esse and, in the same supposit, the esse that belongs directly to it cannot be multiplied. The reason for this is that only one esse for one thing can ever obtain, as St. Thomas says in *S.T.,* III, q. 17, a. 2.

As regards the *second argument,* we answer from Soto himself, in 4, d. 12, q. 1, that it is not correct to conclude that an accident's esse is formally from the esse of substance because an accident's being is the suchness of a being, namely, of substance. That "because" signifies not merely a formal cause or reason, but also a genus of whatever cause, even an extrinsic one. There are as many modes of predicating "because" as there are causal modes, as Aristotle says in *Metaph.,* 5, c. 17. Hence, when Aristotle says that an accident is a being in that it is of substance, he merely means that the entity of an accident is caused by the substance. This, indeed, is true because the substance is an extrinsic material cause of accidents. As for the confirming statement, we answer that the meaning of that "greatest" is that an accident has an esse dependent upon substance in the line of material extrinsic cause, not that it is actual formally through the esse of the substance.

The answer to the *third argument* is that the existence of an accident is the actuality by which an accident is actual in the objective order. This actuality, however, is rightly called "inherence" or "in-existence" [33] * on account of its imperfection and because, of its very nature, it depends on the existence of the subject both for its becoming and for its conservation. For, just as the essence of the accident is to the essence of the substance, so the esse of the accident is to the esse of substance. This dependence, however, is not had to the extent that it cannot be substituted for by God's power, for it is not a dependence in the line of formal causality, as though the esse of the accident is caused by the esse of the substance. Still, the esse of the accident, for its part, retains an intrinsic order to the esse of the substance as to its foundation and root.

*   *   *

For the rest, the arguments from Paul Soncinas [p. 95] in the confirming statement of this position are not of great moment, even though they are considered conclusive by Dominic of Flanders. All these difficulties can be easily solved if one holds that the existence of accidents is indeed distinct by a real formal distinction from the existence of substance, not in the manner in which one thing is really distinct from another thing. This is the same sort of distinction that exists between figure and quantity. According to some, the existence of substance is distinct from substance in no other way than through a real formal distinction, as was said in the third question above. Indeed, through this distinction all the texts in St. Thomas which have been cited can be explained. With this real formal distinction, St. Thomas can be explained. Hence, the second argument, held by M. Soto, is probable.

Regarding the argument based on the accidents which remain in the Eucharist, you will find more than enough answers below in q. 4, art. 1, ad 3. Here, we end our comment on article 4.

NOTES

INTRODUCTION

1. Mondragon is a city in the Basque region of Guipuzcoa. See Espasa-Calpe, S.A., *Enciclopedia Universal Illustrada,* v. 36, 81. *Bañez* will be abbreviated here to Banez. For biographical details, see L. Urbano's introduction to the commentary on the first part which he edited. This is found in the W. C. Brown reprint under the direction of the Dominicans at Dubuque, Iowa, hereafter cited as *In S.T.,* I, (Brown). Biographical data on Banez are based mostly on V. B. de Heredia's findings (see next note below), and the autobiographical narrative Banez gives in *In S.T.,* II-II, Salmantinae, MDLXXXIV, q. 1, a. 7, col. 83. Cf. J. E. de Arteaga, "El Derecho de Gentes en las Obras de F. D. Banez", *Anuario de la Asociacion F. de Vitoria,* Madrid, 1934, 115-168; C. Pozo, *La Teoria del Progreso Dogmatico en los Teologos de la Escuela de Salamanca,* Madrid, 1959, 192-208 on Banez' understanding of the distinction between faith and reason. The forms, *In I, In I-II,* etc. will be used hereafter to cite Banez' commentaries on the various parts of St. Thomas' *Summa Theologiae.* On the various teaching ranks in a mediaeval university, consult M. D. Chenu, translated by Landry & Hughes, *Toward Understanding St. Thomas,* Chicago, 1964; V. Bourke, *Aquinas' Search For Wisdom,* Milwaukee, 1964.

2. V. B. de Heredia, "Valor Doctrinal de las lecturas del P. Banez", *La Ciencia Tomista,* XXXIX, 1929, 79-81. Heredia gives chronological details of Banez'

activities from 1577-1600 in this article. *Idem,* "Actuacion del Maestro D. Banez en la Universidad de Salamanca", *ibid.,* XXV, 1922, 64-78; 208-240; XXVI, 1922, 63-74, 199-223; XXVII, 1923, 40-51, 361-74; XXVIII, 1923, 36-47. *Idem,* "El Maestro D. Banez", *ibid.,* XLVIII, 1933, 26-29, 162-79. *Idem,* "Introduccion", *Commentarios Ineditos a la Prima Secundae,* Madrid, 1948, t. 1, 1-19; t. 2, 1-31; t. 3, 1-14. *Idem,* "Introduccion", *Commentarios Ineditos a la Tercera Parte,* Madrid, 1953, t. 1, 1-30; t. 2, 1-19. For a quick schematic summary of Heredia's conclusions including all the technical details of the different substitutes and their lectures incorporated in the Heredia editions, see M. Midali, *Corpus Christi Mysticum Apud Banez,* Analecta Gregoriana, v. 116, 1962, 19-20. Cf. *In S.T.,* I, (Brown) XVII-XVIII, XXI-XXIII, where the various editions of Banez' works are listed. In his foreword a few pages back, Banez states what one could infer from the dates of publication that his various works were in long periods of preparation before their formal publication. The present translation is made from the 1584 Salamanca edition of which St. Louis University has a copy. In 1934 Luis Urbano had a reprinting of the commentary on the first part. Unfortunately, the plates and much of the edition were destroyed in the Spanish Civil War. Recently, in 1964, W. E. Brown Reprint Library reprinted this Urbano edition up to the 26th question under the direction of the Dominicans at Dubuque, Iowa. The commentary on the first part from question 65 is hard to find. The commentaries on the second and third parts have had fairly recent editions under the direction of V. B. de Heredia and are easily available. Heredia usually has an introductory article to the various volumes explaining the methods used to locate Banez' manuscripts and to work out their chronology and arrangements. Often the lectures of Banez' substitutes at the chair in Salamanca are included in a continuous presentation of the various questions. The reader has to consult these introductory articles and watch the marker pages for the precise beginnings and terminations of these substitute lectures. Harvard has a copy of the commentary on *De Generatione et Corruptione,* and St. Mary of the Lake Seminary at Mundelein, Illinois, has a copy of *De Iustitia et Iure.*

3. Cf. A. Maurer, *Medieval Philosophy,* New York, 1962, 356-67. Hereafter this book is cited as MP. E. Gilson, *Being and Some Philosophers,* Toronto, 1952, 109; 113-14. J. Collins, *History of Modern Philosophy,* Milwaukee, 1956, 456. C. C. Riedl, "Suarez and the Organization of Learning", *Jesuit Thinkers of the Renaissance,* Milwaukee, 1939, 1-62.

4. Cf. L. Rasolo, *Le Dilemme du Concours Divin* (Primat de L'Essence ou Primat de L'Existence) Analecta Gregoriana, 1956. For a survey of Thomists, during the years immediately after Aquinas' death, recognized as Thomists not in terms of the "modern notion of esse," but according to their adherence to doctrines of Aquinas controverted at the time, see F. J. Roensch, *Early Thomistic School,* Iowa, 1964.

5. Cf. C. Fabro, *Participation et Causalité,* Louvain, 1961, 280-315; J. Hegyi, *Die Bedeutung des Seins bei den Klassischen Kommentatoren,* Munchen, 1959; and E. Gilson, *op. cit.,* 74-120. *Idem, History*

of Philosophy in the Middle Ages, New York, 1954, 423-27; 450-72. Hereafter this book is cited as HCPMA. A. Maurer, MP, 347-57.

6. W. N. Clarke, "What is the Really Real?", *Introduction to Metaphysics,* ed. D. A. Drennen, New York, 1963, 449-56. M. Pontifex and I. Trethowan reject the real distinction and understand existence as *assertibility* in *The Meaning of Existence,* New York, 1953. See also Sr. Helen J. John, "Pedro Descoqs: A Devil's Advocate on Essence and Existence", *The Modern Schoolman,* XL, 1, Nov. 1962, 39-54. E. Lapointe, "L' 'esse' Chez Saint Thomas", *Archives de Philosophie,* XXVI, 1963, 59-70. J. Owens, "Common Nature: A Point of Comparison Between Thomistic and Scotistic Metaphysics", *Mediaeval Studies,* XIX, 1957, 1-14. *Idem,* "The Number of Terms in the Suarezian Discussion of Essence and Being", *The Modern Schoolman,* XXXIV, 1957, 147-61. A. Maurer, MP, 353-54. C. Fabro, *op. cit.,* 295-304.

7. For a further development of this point in Banez' doctrine, see B. Llamzon, "The Specification of Esse", *The Modern Schoolman,* XLI, Jan. 1964, 123-43. M. Holloway, "Towards the Fullness of Being", Proceedings, *Am. Jesuit Phil. Assn.,* 1962, 15-37, 57-82. L. Sweeney, *A Metaphysics of Authentic Existentialism,* New Jersey, 1965, 111-27. For the significance of an esse metaphysics, see W. Carlo, "The Role of Essence in Existential Metaphysics", *International Philosophical Quarterly,* December, 1962, 557-90. Sr. Helen J. John, "The Emergence of the Act of Existing in Recent Thomism", *ibid.,* 595-620. L. Eslick, "The Real Distinction", *The Modern Schoolman,* XXXVIII, 1961,

149-60. A. Pegis, *At the Origins of the Thomistic Notion of Man,* New York, 1963. J. Owens, "Unity in a Thomistic Philosophy of Man", *Mediaeval Studies,* XXV, 1963, 54-82. E. Braun, "Le Probleme de L'Esse chez Saint Thomas", *Archives de Philosophie,* XXIII, 1960, 252-89.

8. E. Gilson, *The Christian Philosophy of St. Thomas Aquinas,* tr. L. Shook, New York, 1956, vii, 444.

9. Cf. for instance, J. de Finance, *Existence et Liberté,* Paris, 1955. R. O. Johann, *The Meaning of Love,* Maryland, 1955. F. D. Wilhelmsen, *The Metaphysics of Love,* New York, 1962. *An Etienne Gilson Tribute,* ed. C. J. O'Neil, Milwaukee, 1959.

THE COMMENTARY

1. J. P. Migne, *Patrologiae Latinae,* Paris, 1864, v. 192, 542-46.

2. Cajetan, *In S.T.,* I, q. 3, a. 4 (Leonine ed.), v. 4, 43, III; also q. 28, a. 2, *ibid.,* 323, XIII. *Idem, In De Ente et Essentia,* Taurini, 1934, c. 5, q. 10, 137, and q. 12, 157 where Cajetan mentions A. Trombetta and other Scotists as opposing his position on the questions of multiplying subsistent forms in individuals of a species, and of the real composition between essence and esse. J. Hegyi, "Der Seinsbegriff nach der Lehre des Kardinal Cajetan", *op. cit.,* 107-50. F. Suarez, *Disputationes Metaphysicae,* Paris, 1861, d. XXXI, sec. 1, 11, v. 26, 227, where Suarez mentions Scotus, Henry of Ghent, Soto and "nonulli moderni" as proponents of the formal distinction between esse and essence. See *ibid.,* 228, for those who deny the real distinction outright.

3. On "natural place" see E. A. Burtt, *The Metaphysical Foundations of Modern Science,* New York, 1932, 17-22. F. Copleston, *A History of Philosophy,* Maryland, 1953, v. 3, 157-67. Hereafter this work is cited as HP. A. C. Crombie, *Medieval and Early Modern Science,* New York, 1959, v. 1, 75-98.

4. C. Fabro, *Participation et Causalité,* Louvain, 1961, 282-84 gives an account of the phrase *"esse existentiae."*

5. *formaliter,* i.e., whose precise intelligibility

6. See *In S.T.,* I, q. 3, a. 4 (Leonine ed.), v. 4, 43, III.

7. "What is first understood about every being is not its actual existence. Rather every being is understood through order to actual existence. All creatures, existing and possible, are understood in this way. Although esse itself is not of the creature's essence, nor is it a property or proper accident, still it is first actuality with respect to everything in the essences of creatures or of possible creatures, through order to which all these are called being and are objects of our understanding." Banez, *In S.T.,* III, q. 3, a. 3, 592.

8. J. Collins, *God in Modern Philosophy,* Chicago, 1959, 387, 394, 398-403. E. Sillem, *Ways of Thinking About God,* New York, 1961, 121-25.

9. Cajetan summarizes his thought in *In S.T.,* I, q. 3, a. 4 (Leonine ed.), v. 4, 43, V.

10. P. Hoenen, *Reality and Judgment According to St. Thomas,* Chicago, 1952, 70-72.

11. Cf. F. Suarez, DM, d. XXXI, sec. VII, v. 26, 250-51.

12. See *S.T.*, I, q. 10, a. 5, c, in *Basic Writings of St. Thomas Aquinas,* tr. A. C. Pegis, New York, 1945, 80-81.

13. J. Hegyi, "Der Seinsbegriff im Werk des Johannes Capreolus", *op. cit.,* 7-52. See also note 30 below.

14. L. Eslick, "The Real Distinction", *The Modern Schoolman,* XXXVIII, Jan. 1961, 149-60. On esse and the person, see J. Maritain, *Existence and the Existent,* translated by L. Galantiere and G. B. Phelan, New York, 1956, 70-91.

15. *Opera Omnia,* Parma Reprint, New York, 1949, v. 8, 482. See also, A. Hayen, *La Communication de L'Etre,* Paris, 1959, 108-22. C. Fabro, *op. cit.,* 344-62. Being, says Banez, is above the predicaments and is not reduced to them. In finite beings this means a potency which has act. If this potency then is not reduced to the predicaments, how can one consistently hold that its act is thus reduced?

16. Cajetan, *In S.T.,* I, q. 28, a. 2 (Leonine ed.), v. 4, 323, XIII.

17. See fifth question below for Banez' change of mind on this question.

18. The third argument above argued that esse is an accident, since esse is identical to the duration of a thing and duration belongs to the predicament of quantity or time.

19. On Herveus (Natalis or Nedellec) see Quetif et
    Echard, *Scriptores Ordinis Praedictorium*, Paris,
    1719, v. 1, 2, 533-36. B. Harréau, "Hervé Nedél-
    lec", *Histoire Litteraire de la France*, Paris, 1915,
    XXXIV, 308-51. P. Glorieux, *Repertoire des Maitres
    en Theologie de Paris au XIIIe siecle*, v. 1, 199-206.
    Hereafter this work is cited as *Repertoire*. E. Gilson,
    HCPMA, 747-48. *Lexicon Fur Theologie und
    Kirche*, Freiburg, 1957, v. 5, 284. On Gabriel Biel,
    see F. Ueberweg, *History of Philosophy*, New York,
    1871, tr. G. S. Morris, v. 1, 465. F. Copleston, HP,
    v. 3, 150. A. Maurer, MP, 288, *Lexicon Fur The-
    ologie und Kirche*, v. 2, 454-55. *Dictionnaire de
    Theologie Catholique*, Paris, 1931, v. 2, 1, 814-25.
    On Aureolus, see F. Ueberweg, *op. cit.*, v. 1, 461.
    F. Copleston, HP, v. 3, 29-39. E. Gilson, HCPMA,
    476-80, 777. Also, J. Capreolus, *Defensiones The-
    ologiae*, Turin, 1900, v. 1, 310-11, 317-20, 327-30.
    P. Glorieux, *Repertoire*, v. 2, 244-48. P. Boehner,
    "Notitia Intuitiva of Non-Existens According to
    Peter Aureoli", *Franciscan Studies*, v. 8, 1948, 388-
    416. On Durandus see Quetif et Echard, *op. cit.*, v.
    1, 586-87. *Beitrage zur Geschichte der Philosophie
    des Mittelalters*, J. Koch, Munster, 1927, XXVI, 1,
    5-92. P. Glorieux, *La Litterature Quodlibetique*,
    Paris, 1935, v. 2, 70-75. E. Gilson, HCPMA, 473-
    76, 774-77. F. Copleston, HP, v. 3, 25-28. DTC,
    IV, 2, 1964-66. LTK, v. 3, 612. See also F. Suarez,
    DM, d. XXXI, sec. 12, v. 26, 228.

20. J. D. Scotus, *Opera Omnia* (cum comment. F. Ly-
    cheti et sup. J. Poncii), Paris, 1894, 3 *Sent.*, d. 6,
    q. 1, v. 15, 299-314. A. Alensis, *Summa Theologiae*,
    Quaracchi, 1924, II, Inq. II, tract. 1, q. 1, 513-15.
    Also P. Boehner, *The History of the Franciscan
    School*, Part I, Detroit, 1947, 36-39. P. Glorieux,

Repertoire, v. 1, 15-24. On Augustinus Nipho, see A. Maurer, MP, 341, 422; F. Copleston, HP, v. 3, 221. LTK, v. 7, 1009. On D. de Soto, see V. B. de Heredia, *Domingo de Soto* (Estudio Biografico Documentado) Salamanca, 1960. DTC, XIV, 2, 2423-2431. In his *Commentaria in Librum Praedicamentorum Aristotelis,* Venice, 1574, q. 1 and q. 2, c. 4, 315-17, 354, 362-65, Soto talks about the reduction of esse to the predicaments. He explains the formal distinction in his *Commentaria in Porphyrii Isagogen, Liber Praedicabilium,* Venice, 1574, 208-09. See F. Suarez, DM, d. XXXI, sec. 11, v. 26, 228.

21. On Capreolus, I, d. 8, q. 1, see notes 13 above and 30 below. On Cajetan, *De Ente,* q. 10, see note 2 above. On Ferrara, 2 *Cont. Gent.,* c. 52 (Leonine ed.), v. 13, 388-91. On Barbus Paulus Soncinas, see Quetif et Echard, *op. cit.,* v. 1, 2, 879-80. LTK, v. 9, 873. On Javellus (*Chrysostomo de Casale*) Quetif et Echard, *op. cit.,* v. 2, 104; DTC, VIII, 1, 535-37. Hilarius, *De Trinitate,* lib. 6, *Patrologiae Latinae,* v. 10, 158-98. F. Suarez, DM, d. XXXI, sec. 1, and 3-10, v. 26, 225-27.

22. "The supposit adds something to nature. Now this is not the act of existing. Therefore, it is the mode of the supposit that we are positing, for one can conceive of nothing else on the side of substance which the supposit adds to nature. The confirmation of this is that, before a nature is understood as finally a supposit, it is understood as unterminated and dependent upon another. But, when it is seen to be a supposit, it is determinate and altogether independent. Therefore, the supposit adds to nature a certain real mode by which it is terminated." Banez, *In S.T.,* I, q. 3, a. 3. "I say we are forced to posit

subsistence, because in the context of a reasoned theology we cannot understand the order of the divine persons unless we put personal subsistences by which nature is completed as subsistent and incommunicable. Thus, the theologian argues that created substantial nature ought to be terminated by subsistence by which it is made fully and ultimately subsistent. The metaphysician who assumes that esse is the basic principle of a thing is compelled to say that esse comes to an already terminated nature, since esse belongs to a subsistent, complete nature. Now nature does not subsist completely through individuality. So it has to be constituted through another mode of existing in a complete and incommunicable existence. This we call subsistence, suppositality, or personality. It follows that the proper effect of subsistence is to complete and terminate an incomplete nature so that it may exist." *Idem, In S.T.,* III, q. 2, a. 2, 494-95. "It must be said that personality is really distinct from the act of existing, as also from essence, and that the act of existing itself is as the act of both, namely, of essence and personality. It is the act of personality first and immediately, and then of essence." *Idem, In S.T.,* III, q. 4, a. 2, 148-49. ". . . esse comes to nature not as that which has esse. It is the person or the supposit which has esse. However, it is true that the act of existing is the act of the nature and the supposit. It is the first and immediate act of the supposit, and the act of the nature only mediately." *Idem, In S.T.,* III, q. 4, a. 2. See B. S. Llamzon, "Suppositral and Accidental Esse in Banez", *The New Scholasticism,* XXXIX, 2, April, 1965, 170-88.

23. See note 19 above.

24. See J. Owens, "Common Nature", *Mediaeval Studies,* XIX, 1957, 1-14. A. O'Brien, "Duns Scotus on the Distinction Between Essence and Existence", *The New Scholasticism,* XXXVIII, 1964, 61-77. M. Grajewski, *The Formal Distinction of D. Scotus,* Washington, D.C., 1944, 87. A. Wolter, *The Transcendentals in Duns Scotus,* New York, 1946, 24-5. E. Bettoni, *Duns Scotus,* translated by B. Bonansea, Washington, D.C., 1961, 65-6.

25. J. D. Scotus, *Opera Omnia,* Paris, 1894, 4 *Sent.,* d. 1, q. 1, v. 16, 12-99, especially 55-8 (cum comment. A. Hiquaei). F. Suarez, *DM,* d. XXXI, sec. 13, 19-23, 304-06.

26. Dionysius, *De Divinis Nominibus,* c. 5, *Patrologiae Graecae,* v. 3, 815-26. Banez' quote from Aristotle is inaccurate. See *The Basic Works of Aristotle,* ed. R. McKeon, New York, 1941, p. 1070, where Aristotle talks of the father, not God, as conferring existence on his children.

27. "Scotus and others say that the essences of things which are signified in such expressions as 'man is an animal' have esse from eternity, not indeed *esse existentiae,* but *esse essentiale et quidditativum.* In *Metaphysics,* IX, q. 4, Soncinas cites this point. Thus, these authors say, since there is a twofold esse in man, quidditative and essential, and existential, man is from eternity with regard to his essential and quidditative esse. Thus, as some hold that God by His absolute power could conserve essence without existence, so these others hold that essence *is* from all eternity even without existence. For the explanation of q. 3, a. 4, ad 2 of St. Thomas above, note

that esse is taken in three ways: *esse essentiale et quidditativum, esse existentiae,* and still another which signifies the connection and truth of the proposition. This connection is fundamentally in the object and formally in the intellect. Secondly, note that *esse existentiae* does two things with regards to *esse essentiae.* First, it makes *esse essentiae* to be *in actu,* whereas before it was *in potentia.* Thus, man, before existing, is a potential being, not actual. Secondly, it makes *esse essentiae* a created thing, for, before its existence, it was a creatable, not a created being, for creation is terminated in something which exists, as St. Thomas teaches in *De Potentia,* q. 3, a. 5, ad 2. Thus, real being is divided in the first instance into uncreated Being, which is existence by essence, and into created being, which has esse, not by its essence, but through existence which is accidental to that essence. Finally, notice with Cajetan in *De Ente,* c. 4, q. 6, that real being is twofold: one, as contrasted to a being produced by the intellect; two, as contrasted to the non-existent. First conclusion. The essences of things are not from eternity, either regarding their actual or their quidditative and essential existence. God alone exists from eternity. In *De Potentia,* q. 3, a. 5, ad 2, St. Thomas expressly says that essence without existence is nothing. Secondly, that quidditative esse, which they say is from eternity, is either produced by God or not. If it is so produced, then it has existence, since God's production terminates in an existing esse. If it is not so produced, then we have a being without any relation to God. Finally, if this position were true, creation would be impossible, since creation is the production of the whole being, while these things would have been existing quidditatively from eternity; thus they cannot be produced in the totality of their being.

Second conclusion. Animal is of the essence of man from eternity. But the esse in this is not an absolute one in the creature, but only a relative one, for it is esse in potency. Third conclusion. If that word *is* refers to the truth of the proposition 'Man is an animal', then this is not eternal, except in the divine intellect, for only the divine intellect is from eternity. From these conclusions, it follows that the essences of things, before they exist, are real beings in the sense that a real being is contrasted to a being of the mind, a fictitious being; this is not true in the second sense." Banez, *In S.T.,* I, q. 10, a. 3; *In S.T.,* III, q. 17, a. 2. Also, P. Hoenen, *op. cit.,* 52-62.

28. See L. Molina, *In S.T.,* I, q. 23, a. 4, Lugduni, 1623, especially 48-54. *Idem, Concordia Liberi Arbitrii,* Paris, 1876, d. XXV, 147-52, especially 150; d. XXVI and appendix, 147-71, especially 166-67. F. Suarez, *DM,* d. XIII, 2, 20, v. 25, 605, and d. XXII, 2, 20, v. 25, 815, where Suarez cites and approves of this precise text in Scotus and names other "Thomistae" of the same persuasion.

29. Ferrara, 2 *Cont. Gent.,* c. 21, 54, 55 (Leonine ed.), v. 13, 314-20, 392-93, 395-402 respectively.

30. On Gerard of Bologna, see E. Gilson, HCPMA, 483, 780. P. Glorieux, *Repertoire,* v. 2, 336-37. *Idem, La Littérature Quodlibetique,* v. 2, 94-5. Henry of Ghent, *Quodlibeta,* Louvain, 1961, v. 2, fol. 556-59. J. Capreolus, *Defensiones,* I, d. 8, q. 1, on Henry of Ghent, v. 1, 311, 315, 321-22; on Gerard of Bologna, *ibid.,* 315-16, 322-25. See N. Wells, "Capreolus on Essence and Existence", *The Modern Schoolman,* XXXVII, 1960, 1-24. *Idem,* "Suarez, Historian and Critic of the Modal Distinction", *The New Scholasti-*

cism, XXXVI, 1962, 419-44. *Idem,* "Descartes and the Scholastics Briefly Revisited", *ibid.,* XXXV, 1961, 172-90.

31. "There is, in nature, a passive potency for the reception of fire; thus, there will also be an active potency to induce fire. To every passive potency there is a corresponding active potency." Banez, *Commentaria In De Generatione et Corruptione,* Venetiis, 1596, 36D. This work is cited hereafter as *In D.G.E.C.* "If we take generation and corruption as actions, an action being that by which something is generated and its opposite corrupted, then identically the generation of one being is the corruption of another." *Ibid.,* 52A. "A man effects the production of a man and the union of the soul with matter, for he disposes matter to that final stage which immediately precedes the introduction of the new form. And man has the power to dispose matter determinatively to the esse of the rational soul, because he himself has a rational soul which has this power." *Ibid.,* 109AB. "What is effected through generation or through alteration is neither matter nor form but the composite." *Ibid.,* 159E. "In everything, the generation of one being is the corruption of another. No total corruption of a substance can take place without a generation in the same matter." *Ibid.,* 31E, 230A. "The term of generation is neither the essence nor the existence of a being, but the supposit as subsisting and existing in nature." *In S.T.,* III, q. 17, a. 2.

32. "The agent is the principle of motion and is quite different from a formal or a final cause. An agent acts in the strict sense. A final cause acts only in a metaphorical sense. The desire for health is not effi-

cient except metaphorically." Banez, *In D.G.E.C.,*
262A. "All things which can be generated and corrupted have matter; therefore, they have form since
matter is for, and never devoid of, form. Now this
form is a final cause in the physical order because it
is on account of it that the efficient cause acts, for
form and species is the end of action and of the intention of the natural agent." *In D.G.E.C.,* 393E.
"The end, the desirable, the good are of the same
intelligibility. A sick man does not desire health as
an idea of the mind, but as existing in the real order,
in his body." *In S.T.,* I-II, q. 1, a. 1. "The explanation for finality (*ratio finalizandi*) is the esse of a
thing which is the end, just as the explanation for
activity is the form of the agent . . . now the condition for the end is to be in the intention, just as
the condition for the agent is to be an individual subsistent. The reason why health is desired and is desirable is not its esse in the mind, but its esse in the
actual order, in one's own body. And so the intelligibility of finality and end is the esse of health in
the actual order. It is clear, however, that health
could never be desired unless it is known. Thus, to
be known is a condition for finality. Furthermore, it
is clear that the desirable moves what is at rest.
Therefore, to be in process, which is to exist in actual dependence upon the agent, is neither the end
nor the condition for the end. Otherwise, it would
not be moving what is at rest. But the end of generation and the form of what is generated are numerically identical; hence, one can admit a certain iden-
tification between process and end." *In S.T.,* I-II,
q. 1, a. 1.

33. "The essence of an accident, as related to its subject,
is not *actual in-existence.* In the Eucharist, for in-

stance, this does not obtain. Furthermore, what is pointed to here is existence which is not the essence of any creature. Now neither can aptitudinal inherence be the essence of an accident. First, this still refers to esse, and actual or aptitudinal esse simply is not essential to any finite being. Second, the ability to exist by itself does not pertain to the essence of substance; hence, neither does the ability to inhere pertain to the essence of an accident. Third, if what we hold here is false, then the questions "what is it?" and "is it?" would be one and the same question as regards an accident, for the question "is it?" refers to aptitudinal existence. The essence of an accident is rather this: to be a thing to which existence-in-another is proportionate, as St. Thomas teaches in *S.T.*, III, q. 67, a. 1, ad 2, and *Quodlibetales,* 9, a. 4, ad 2." *In D.G.E.C.,* 72CD. "Any kind of accident may be considered in two ways. One is to see it precisely as an accident with an essence ordered to a subject. This is what is commonly referred to by the saying 'the existence of an accident is in-existence', that is, the essence of an accident is taken with respect to its inherence in a subject. This does not mean the inherence itself is its essence. Its essence is to be a thing to which existence-in-another is proportionate. Two, one may consider an accident as essentially of this or that kind, for instance, heat, whiteness, etc. Thus considered, an accident's specific difference does not arise from its order of inherence in a subject. It arises either from itself absolutely, as in the case of whiteness, or from its order to something extrinsic, as in the case of a science, or by proportion to the nature of its subject, as health in a man is differentiated from health in a horse." *In D.G.E.C.,* 72CD.